Reviews

The world of B2B sales is changing at a rate never seen in the past, but those wanting to be successful must still master the traditional basics. This reference handbook that will prove invaluable to new salespeople and those looking to refresh their skills.

> – Tony J. Hughes, Managing Director at RSVPselling Pty Ltd. Keynote Speaker, Sales Improvement Consultant, Bestselling Author & Award Winning Blogger (Australia)

This is a book that provides good, common sense insights into B2B selling. It is a practical and compelling handbook for anyone new to sales, or those more experienced looking to refresh their knowledge on sales basics.

> – John Smibert; Founder, Sales Masterminds Australasia – Speaker, Author, Consultant, Trainer (Australia)

Follow Wayne Moloney's thinking and you will sell more, guaranteed!

> – Bernadette McClelland, CEO 3 Red Folders. Speaker, Author, Facilitator and Executive Sales Coach (Australia)

Wayne Moloney has demonstrated once again that Selling is both a masterful and honourable craft…if this information is applied diligently, vast improvements and results will ensue.

> – Sean Patrick; CEO, SPT Ltd. Sales Enablement and New Business Development Consultant (United Kingdom)

This book demonstrates the bottom line of sales skills and mindset that are essential to be successful in B2B sales.

> – Peter Strohkorb; CEO, Peter Strohkorb Consulting International P/L - International Author, Speaker, Mentor (Australia)

Your Roadmap to Achieving Sales Success is an excellent and inspiring read which aims at empowering salespeople to influence buying decisions.

> – Kitty Scheperman; VP Sales at Improving Sales & Benchmarkingsales.eu. Improving Sales and Marketing B2B Development. (Netherlands)

This book will give any sales person a thorough grounding on what you need to know – and know in-depth.

> – Steve Hall, Managing Director at Executive Sales Coaching Australia. Keynote Speaker, Executive Sales Coach, Storyteller (Australia)

YOUR ROADMAP TO
ACHIEVING SALES
SUCCESS

*Compiled from over
40 years of practical
sales experience*

WAYNE MOLONEY

This is an IndieMosh book brought to you by
MoshPit Publishing an imprint of Mosher's Business Support Pty Ltd
PO BOX 147
Hazelbrook NSW 2779
www.indiemosh.com.au

First published 2018 © Wayne Moloney

The moral right of the author has been asserted.

Cataloguing-in-Publication entry is available from the National Library of Australia:
http://catalogue.nla.gov.au/

Title: Your Roadmap to Achieving Sales Success
Author: Moloney, Wayne
ISBN: 978-1-925595-34-5 (paperback)
          978-1-925529-81-4 (ebook – epub)
          978-1-925529-82-1 (ebook – mobi)

"And old Dave, he'd go up to his room, y'understand, put on his green velvet slippers—I'll never forget—and pick up his phone and call the buyers, and without leaving his room, at the age of eighty-four, he made his living. And when I saw that, I realized that selling was the greatest career a man could want."

Arthur Miller (1915—2005),
***Death of a Salesman*, 1949.**

Contents

Foreword...9

Preface 13

Acknowledgements...15

Introduction..17

Section 1—Profiling the Successful Salesperson............................23

    Chapter One: Taking on a Positive Attitude 29

    Chapter Two: Knowing What Sales Professionals Know 37

    Chapter Three: Sharpening Your Communications Skills 46

    Chapter Four: Keeping Time on Your Side 55

    Chapter Five: Taking Charge of Yourself 69

    Chapter Six: Committing Yourself to Teamwork 79

    Chapter Seven: Planning for Your Success 91

Section 2—Understanding Relationship Selling..............................109

    Chapter Eight: Tried and Tested Relationship Selling 115

    Chapter Nine: Relationship Selling and Social Media 129

    Chapter Ten: Your Personal Brand 139

Section 3—The Sales Cycle...145

    Stage One: Lead Generation..154

    Stage Two: Approach and Qualify...165

    Stage Three: Identify Needs...186

    Stage Four: Formulate and present solution 192

    Stage Five: Provide Answers 209

    Stage Six: Confirm the Sale...213

    Stage Seven: Implementation 216

    Stage Eight: Follow-up and start again 217

Epilogue: Miscellaneous thoughts to help you become
    a better salesperson..219

About the Author 233

Foreword

This book does not break new ground and deliver the reader with new sales methodologies.

Your Roadmap to Achieving Sales Success is a book that provides good, common sense insights into B2B selling. It is a practical and compelling handbook for anyone new to sales, or those more experienced looking to refresh their knowledge on sales basics.

Selling is not easy. And it can be a formidable challenge for somebody new to sales—and for some not so new—to learn how to succeed.

It is tough to compete in sales. It is tough to get the attention of customers. More and more buyers do not value salespeople as much as in previous years for two reasons; firstly their experience is that many salespeople do not add value and just want to push their product or service, and secondly, they now believe they can access all the information they need to make buying decisions without the assistance of salespeople.

Yet despite these challenges, new salespeople with the right development and coaching can, and do, succeed. They learn how to help customers achieve the outcomes the customer is looking for in their business and private lives—and they learn how to do this with focus on the customers needs—and without a primary intent of selling their product.

So, how can a new salesperson—or even a more mature salesperson—hone their skills and develop the capability to influence customers to buy from them?

One way is to read sales books. There is a multitude available.

However, as the title of this book promises, few books provide the clear '*roadmap to achieving sales success*' that this book does in such a concise handbook format. It cleverly covers all the important areas of sales and applies the latest thinking and methods, in a step by step process.

The book is great for an individual salesperson as a personal sales handbook. Even more significant, is that it's an excellent resource for assisting sales managers in coaching their team members. It provides many practical exercises for the reader to undertake—activities that will reinforce the lessons.

Section 1 of the book provides a profile of a successful salesperson.

This is a critical section for new salespeople and brings together all the leading thinking of many of the sales masters of the past and present. It starts with how to develop the right attitude for success and then covers the knowledge and communications skills needed. It demonstrates how to influence others in a positive and constructive way. Time management, teamwork and planning are all covered in a easy to learn manner. Key to success, as Moloney emphasises, is that as salespeople we must take charge of ourselves. He shows us that we need to become a leader and a manager "across the domains of our life—self, home, work and community"—and he outlines how.

Section 2 addresses how to be a successful relationship salesperson.

Important to note is that Moloney focuses on creating customer value as the key determinant of building a positive relationship.

This covers older tried and tested methods as well as modern methods such as the application of 'social selling'.

Section 3 then outlines various aspects of the end-to-end sales cycle, with particular emphasis on how it needs to adapt to and align with the buyer's journey. We must be helping the customer buy—and not dictating to the customer how they should buy.

Finally the book's Epilogue provides you with many tools and resources to help you elevate your professionalism in sales.

I close by asking you to get in the right frame of mind to get the most from this book.

Remember selling is helping and giving. The word 'sell' is derived from an old English/Germanic word 'Sellan' or 'Sellen' which means 'to give'.

Your underlying intent when selling will determine your level of success and satisfaction with your sales career. If your intent is to close orders and make a lot of commission, your customers will see through that and will not trust you. If your intent is to give, to help, to create value for the customer in their context and from their perspective, your customers will trust you and you will succeed.

Wishing you every success in leveraging the gold in this book to create value for your customers—and get your share of value in return.

John Smibert—Founder, Sales Masterminds Australasia

February 2018

Preface

Just as life has been quickly and irrevocably changed by information and communications technology, so the sales profession has been disrupted and has been going through a significant transformation as a result. More informed, connected customers are driving a very worthwhile change to a more professional and principled, smart and mutually valuable way of engaging in the buying and selling process.

While I recognise that change brings challenges; as someone who has been a professional in sales and marketing, management and business development for over four decades, I believe the changed sales environment of today is deeply exciting.

The ability to consistently challenge your clients and yourself to achieve value-driven, relationship-rooted sales in today's wildly competitive and flighty marketplace is literally separating the wheat from the chaff. And, that's good news for sales as a profession.

What hasn't changed is this: 'Nothing happens until someone makes a sale.'

Those who put themselves on the frontline to find and connect with the people who will benefit from their company's products or services are the vital drivers of business. There's one word in that last sentence that denotes the difference though. That word is 'benefit'. In the past, salespeople looked to anyone who may be persuaded in the moment to want their product or service; and this gave rise to clichéd slick, 'fly-by-night' salesman of years gone by. Sales has matured significantly since then, and today, it is a career chosen by highly educated individuals who deliver sustainable solutions, benefits and value to their clearly-targeted customers.

Over my early career, I was lucky to have experienced guides and mentors on my side to help me solve business problems and develop myself. I know that not everyone with great selling potential has access to an excellent mentor. This book is designed to be the next best thing. I am not delivering game-changing, new selling concepts—I am giving you a trusted roadmap to achieving success in sales, full of relevant, tried and tested advice, expertise and tools.

I have distilled more than 40 years of my business management, sales and training experience and expertise gained across a diverse range of industries in Australian, Asian and European markets into this roadmap to help you realise your full potential as high performance sales professional.

Good luck!

Wayne Moloney
Blue Mountains, New South Wales
February 2018

Acknowledgements

My career in Sales started after, as a rather over-confident mechanical engineer trainee, I had a rather robust discussion with my boss who decided it was best for me to find another path in life. Without this 'motivation', I may never have discovered a career that has been exciting, frustrating, enormous fun and very rewarding. So to this person, who shall remain anonymous, I say a heartfelt "Thanks'.

On a more serious note, I thank my wife Gela and my family for their support and understanding over the years. While Sales is a great and satisfying career, it is not without challenges and pressures on your personal life.

I would also like to thank the many people, too numerous to mention, who helped me continually develop as a salesperson throughout my career—my sales managers, clients, peers, those who said "no" to my proposals and my competitors—each and every one of these people helped me grow and better understand what was needed to be successful.

More recently I have enjoyed the company of some great thought-leaders in sales and was humbled to be invited to become a member of Sales Masterminds Australasia. I thank John Smibert for his vision and efforts in establishing this group, and for the support he has provided me on both a personal and professional level over the past several years.

Introduction

There are three essential concepts that underpin this *Roadmap to Achieving Sales Success* that I am going to introduce to you, and then you will find them interwoven through the entire guide. They are:

1. Selling is about people, not products—Here's a fact: people buy things all the time, but they hate being sold to by incompetent salespeople. In our modern world, the salesperson's role as an influential provider of information in order to 'make a sale' is over. By the time you meet a prospect they will most likely know as much about your product and your business as you know about them. They are also more likely to trust what others say on the internet about your product and business than they will trust what you have to say about them, at least initially. Today's successful sales professional, especially in the B2B environment, knows that what they have to do is deliver value, not extract money. In this context, the financial transaction is a natural progression of a developed relationship.

"It used to be that people needed products to survive.
Now products need people to survive."
Nicholas Johnson (1934—~), American author, former
Federal Communications Minister and teacher of law

---

2. Consistent success in sales is about having a *lean* approach to following an organised sales process, and is not left to chance or luck—I've known many very successful sales professionals, and they all have some things in common. They are extremely well-organised people who take a strategic view of sales. They work to understand the business of their prospect or customer. They look for solutions to problems or opportunities to improve performance. They are completely focused on identifying and delivering what their prospect or customer sees as value—That value might include providing insights into market trends or identifying opportunities the prospect is not aware of. They plan for their success. They follow a clear process and track their progress with their prospects and customers throughout a defined sales cycle that they ensure is aligned to the buyer's process. Every step of the way, they pause to reflect, to assess and to analyse so they can reduce waste in the sales process and ensure that they keep focused on the real opportunities.

3. Your success as a sales professional is wholly reliant on you, your attitude and your behaviours, and will not be affected by any external circumstances—Just as many of us can be the proverbial 'author of our own misfortune,' we also have the power to be the 'creators of our own fortune'—especially in the sales profession where earnings are unlimited. With a positive attitude, a sales professional can keep making sales and gaining customers even in troubled economic times. With superb relationship skills, a sales professional can inspire others to turnaround their performance in a struggling organisation. With an unwavering focus on being successful a sales professional can push through any adversity and achieve their personal and work goals.

"Sales are contingent upon the attitude of the salesperson—not the attitude of the prospect."
Dr Tony Alessandra, American best-selling author, entrepreneur and motivational speaker.

There are times in this book I refer to *relationship* and *solutions-based* selling. Many sales commentators now denigrate these terms, but I strongly believe both are still relevant. It is the definition and understanding of each that is important.

Relationship selling is not about kowtowing to your prospect or customer—meeting their every demand to please them. It is much more complex than that. Professional B2B selling is about delivering value to your clients. It is about challenging the way they currently do business and helping them find new ways to grow or address problems. It is about understanding how to help your client be more successful. This can only be achieved if you *develop a strong relationship* with those within your client organisation who are willing to make decisions on change. In challenging the way an organisation currently does business, you will be *delivering solutions*—not just products or services.

It is important as we work together throughout this book that these understandings of relationship and solution are borne in mind.

This roadmap has been developed to help salespeople and business owners who are responsible for sales, transform themselves into successful sales professionals. I hope it will inspire you to operate at a higher and more fulfilling level that not only leads to you enjoying a successful career in sales, but leads you to being part of 'raising the bar' for the whole sales profession.

Through adopting the principles I share in this book, you will:

- gain in-depth insights and understanding of the essential attitudes and behaviours of a sales professional
- reflect on, and recognise the ways in which your own interpersonal abilities, styles and attitudes impact on others
- make use of valuable, practical business tools so that you can follow a lean, focused and well-managed sales process
- learn how you can enhance your leadership and self-management skills, and use them in service to achieving success in sales

I invite you now to join me and dig deeper into this interactive guide to learn more about how to operate as a sales professional and implement a sales process that will lead you to greater success. The chapters are arranged in sections to build your expertise sequentially; however you can also use this book by exploring the chapters in the order that seems most relevant to your needs. To facilitate deeper self-learning, I have included some practical and reflective exercises that you would experience if you were able to attend a sales training program. I encourage you to keep a notebook handy and work through these exercises; there is no doubt you'll get more value from doing them than by just reading them.

As this is an interactive learning experience, it makes sense for you to personalize it as much as possible. So before we go further, take a moment to reflect and to set some personal goals that you would like to achieve as a result of reading this book.

A personal SWOT analysis

What are my current strengths as a salesperson?	What are my current weaknesses as a salesperson?

Your Strengths and Weaknesses are attributes within your control

What opportunities are there for me to further develop as a salesperson?	What are threats to my further development as a salesperson?

Environmental factors are external; they are outside your direct control

I think my greatest challenge in being an effective salesperson is:

_____

_____

_____

_____

I think my greatest attribute in being an effective salesperson is:

_____

_____

_____

_____

As a result of working through this book, I want to develop my skills as a salesperson in the following areas:

_____

_____

_____

_____

Whether you are a newly appointed salesperson needing to learn skills and methodologies, or you've been in the role for quite some time and feel the need to boost performance, this book will assist you in your efforts to become a successful sales professional. Let's get to work!

Section 1
Profiling the Successful Salesperson

The profile of the successful salesperson today is in sharp contrast to the stereotype of the back-slapping 'snake-oil' salesperson of the past. Many well-educated and very qualified people choose a career in selling because of the freedom it offers, as well as the high levels of satisfaction and earning potential. High performance sales professionals are perceived as valuable problem-solvers and partners when it comes to their clients' business development; and they can command salaries equal to those of doctors and lawyers.

Similarly, the way that successful salespeople go about selling couldn't be more different from the overwhelming and manipulative techniques commonly portrayed by the more traditional caricature of a salesperson. The reality is that people buy from people— mostly, frequently and reliably, they buy from people they know and like, who they also trust and respect. Therefore, achieving success in sales is far less about how assertive and outgoing you can be; and far more about how intuitive you are and effective at helping individuals and companies meet their business objectives

---

"Trust is like paper, once it's crumpled, it can never be perfect again."
Anonymous

There is a general belief in modern selling that people 'buy' the salesperson before they buy a product or service or company image. Far from employing bamboozling techniques, the successful salesperson is finely tuned into the subtleties of human interaction and is committed to authentic engagement with their prospects and customers.

Although this book is primarily focused on B2B selling, the need to build trust and to recognize the uniqueness of a customer is also applicable in varying degrees in B2C sales, both at a transactional and a higher level. It is how this is developed and nurtured that is key.

For example, one Saturday I bought a new computer. The guy at the Apple store asked questions to understand why I wanted what I did, and then gave me the pros and cons of the decision I was making. He was very helpful and he succeeded in developing a level of trust. However, on the Sunday when I was trying to set up my new Mac, I experienced difficulties and wanted assistance over the phone. I rang the store, but unfortunately the person who answered the phone had little concern for my plight. She said she couldn't help as she 'couldn't see my screen', and if I wasn't happy, I had two options: I could bring it back for a refund or bring it in and someone would help me set it up. I knew that all I needed was for someone to give me an explanation that was entirely possible over the phone. As it turned out, after I worked out what was happening on my own, I easily fixed the issue. If I had encountered the attitude of this woman on the Saturday when I came to make the purchase, there's no doubt I would have walked out and taken my business elsewhere.

While the 'fast-talking salesman' caricature has been nothing more than a joke for true sales professionals, it has had a cultural impact that particularly affects those who need to step into a sales role in order to drive their business's success. It is not uncommon for people to feel deeply uncomfortable, and perhaps, embarrassed about selling to others. If this rings any bells for you, then note that it is a significant barrier to sales success. If this is not something that you can overcome by reframing how a salesperson needs to be and what they need to do to be successful, then it is important to seriously consider whether sales is the right career for you. On the other hand, if it is a necessity for you to be the salesperson in your own business, then you need to put aside this 'phobia' in the short term so that you can as quickly as possible get into a position to engage a dedicated professional to take on the role of sales; someone who loves what they do.

In this section, you will gain insights into the characteristics, attributes and disciplines that make the difference between a salesperson who is just getting by, and one who consistently and smartly optimises opportunities to deliver value to their customers, again and again.

"Everyone lives by selling something."
Robert Louis Stevenson (1850—1894), Scottish novelist,
poet, essayist, and travel writer.

Chapter One
Taking on a Positive Attitude

Your attitude is everything

Whether you aim to have a successful sales career, or be a world-class athlete or a brilliant banker for that matter, your attitude sets your focus and determines your outcomes.

By its very nature, success is positive; and it stands to reason that what different successful people all have in common is their positive attitude towards whatever it is they are doing that makes them so successful.

Therefore, you have to start out on the road to success in sales with a relentlessly positive attitude to selling.

"In order to succeed, we must first believe that we can."
Nikos Kazantzakis (1883—1957), Greek writer and
philosopher

One of the most effective ways to cultivate that positive attitude is to start by perceiving your role from the buyer's perspective. There are two great motivators of buying. The first is 'buying for gain'—you pay to get something you perceive will give you an advantage or benefit. The second is 'buying for pain'—you pay to get something you perceive will solve your problem or soothe your troubles. In both scenarios, the salesperson is a benefactor helping people to get something that will be good for them. It is an inherently positive role to play, and a solid foundation for perceiving yourself and your work as making a valuable contribution.

People with a positive attitude are compelling to others. Negative people inevitably drag us down and repel us; but most people naturally gravitate towards, feel encouraged by and value people who 'look on the bright side of life.'

Optimism underpins a positive attitude

People who easily maintain their positive attitudes are the optimists of the world. Optimism is a lot more than putting on a cheery face; it is a deep worldview or a fixed mental outlook that is based on expecting the best. Research studies have shown that practising optimism doesn't just increase a person's day-to-day happiness and satisfaction; it impacts on a lifetime, improving physical health and mental well-being, and promoting longevity. Optimism drives a person towards their goal by enabling them to view obstacles as opportunities to find better routes, and setbacks as chances to learn and gain valuable experience. While pessimists might argue that optimists are out of tune with 'reality'; the complete opposite is true. Optimists are so engaged with their reality, that they understand that they are creating it and they take responsibility for their experiences. This allows them to move on quickly from situations that don't work well for them and to find new ways of being and doing that do deliver the outcomes they want.

"A pessimist sees difficulty in every opportunity. An optimist sees opportunity in every difficulty."
Sir Winston Churchill (1874-1965), Wartime Prime
Minister of United Kingdom

Successful salespeople are optimistic, and this enables them to be:

- more friendly

- more resilient

- more determined

- more accountable

- more confident

- more successful

- more resourceful

- more trustworthy

Are successful salespeople extroverts?

A long-held assumption is that extroverted people naturally do better in sales than others. Certainly, the profession does attract a large share of extroverts; and many businesses, in years past, have defined an extroverted nature as a hiring criterion for salespeople. But it is arguable that an extroverted nature is an automatic advantage in selling. While extroverts are seen as sociable, friendly and gregarious, some may express a shadow side where they are so needy to have all the attention on themselves that they are too focused on getting what they want from others and they talk more about themselves than they listen. It is also not uncommon for successful salespeople to have introverted natures. Not all introverts are shy; many, like myself might be 'natural loners' who also have the well-developed confidence to engage authentically and successfully with others.

Your attitude determines the type of salesperson you are

Whether you are a small business owner driving sales to make your company successful or a member of a sales team, your attitude will determine which of these defined levels of salesmanship you operate at.

Have a look at these descriptions, reflect and identify the type of salesperson you are at this time:

1. The Order Taker—this salesperson makes themselves available as they wait for a customer to ask if they can buy. If they are friendly, efficient and effective at taking the order, the customer, who made the decision to buy all on their own, might like them; but they're unlikely to regard them, or remember them for delivering any value to them. And as on-line sales become more and more the norm, the future of this style of salesperson is certainly in jeopardy.

2. The Techo—this salesperson tries to impress the customer by displaying their detailed technical knowledge of their product or service. They focus on telling the customer as much as possible about the dazzling features, and miss the point that customers buy benefits and solutions; not features. They may be the kind of person who wants to show-off their knowledge, often at the expense of the customer, making them feel less knowledgeable. I've often come across this type of salesperson in technical fields, and have recently also experienced it in the horticultural industry. The Techo needs to be aware that they risk isolating and offending customers, and they may well put in a lot of effort for slim results. They also need to be aware that with the level of information now available on-line, their prospects and customers will see them of even less value in future buyer's journeys.

3. The 'I Can Do it All'—this salesperson promises the customer the world just to get the sale in the moment. They may succeed in getting a first sale but they have little to no chance of building the on-going, trusted relationships that are so necessary for the repeat business that underpin a successful sales career. Therefore, this type of salesperson is in it for the short term. This salesperson also has little consideration for the rest of their organisation. They often sell 'futures' or products and services at the limit of its capability, making it difficult for others to deliver, implement and maintain. They often tend to be so focused their own achievement that they fail to be mindful of the fact that a collaborative process is needed across all areas of a business in order to increase its revenue and profits.

4. The Value Creator—this salesperson makes the effort to get to know the customer and understand their needs and problems. They focus on the benefits of their product or service, and thoroughly think through how they can provide a worthwhile solution that is *valued* by the customer. They position themselves well to genuinely build rapport and trust, to develop and maintain relationships, and to act as an advisor to the customer who *adds tangible value*. In the role of a trusted and valued advisor, they actively consider ways of helping their prospect or customer do their business better. They are confident enough to challenge customers to think differently and to help them shift the status quo. They are operating on the level of a sales professional.

Many years ago, I opened a branch of a start-up (or maybe I should say upstart) data communications company. In those days, data communications was considered a bit of a 'black art' (in fact, products were referred to as 'black boxes'); and unless you had a technical background you were considered unlikely to succeed in sales. I had no technical background in data communications—I was a mechanical engineer who had a passion for sales and business development! My competitors made it clear to the market that they thought my company was mad appointing someone who didn't know the technology, and they implied that I would not be able to properly support clients. At the end of 12 months, I had established a strong base on which the company could grow its operations and was about to take up a new troubleshooting role at a different branch, I was invited by a computer user group to a farewell. At this meeting, the President of the group, now a client of mine, announced to the audience: "When Wayne came to Brisbane, his competitors tried to convince us he'd fail as he had no technical background. Well 12 months later, I am here to say that Wayne knows f-all about the technology, but he does know how it applies to our business, and that's a refreshing change."

In this period of my career, I also had a client who saw me as a 'trusted and valued advisor'. So much so, that if a competitor approached with an option we had not discussed, he would contact me to see if it should be considered. If it was right for his business, I always told him so. That led to me having a loyal client, convinced I had his best intentions at heart, which I did, and his network ended up totally managed by my company.

Are you solutions-focused?

Here's a simple reflective exercise, which box do you tick?

Solutions-focused:	Problem-focused:
• You are continually learning about the markets of your clients and how your products or services may provide value and competitive advantage • You look for cause and how to prevent it happening • You seek clarity • You take ownership • You are accountable • You are responsible	• You look to address the immediate issue • You do not look at what a client could be achieving if they did things differently • You blame others • You make excuses • You are in denial • You are easily frustrated • You give up easily

What stands in the way of being solutions-focused?

The biggest culprit is the fear of failure, commonly recognised as 'FUD'—Fear, Uncertainty and Doubt.

Fear paralyses you and makes it impossible to sell well. Ongoing anxieties may be rooted in lack of self-esteem and fear of rejection.

"Never stop because you are afraid—you are never so likely to be wrong."
Fridtjof Nansen (1861—1930) Norwegian explorer, Nobel Peace Prize winner

---

Of course, what you focus on tends to show up and these are some of the forms failure may take in your life:

- failure to prepare
- failure to make a sale
- failure to make a quota
- failure to keep a job

How you react to your fears will determine your fate. Here are 5 typical reactions to fear that trip you up:

- deny it
- avoid it
- make an excuse
- blame others
- quit

But, there is another way. If you react positively to your fears, they won't turn into failures. Here's how to turn your fears into life lessons:

- look at a failure as an event from which you can learn and grow

- understand the 'why' and find a solution
- list possible opportunities
- ask yourself: "what have I learned?" and try again don't mope around with other failures, find people who are succeeding and hang around them

---

"7 times down, 8 times up"
Japanese proverb

Holding back because of fear of failure is sure to lead to failure in sales. Consider this:

Nearly half of sales cycles end without the salesperson asking for the order—you won't get the sale if you don't ask for it!

NO doesn't always mean NO!!! How does this work? Sales are rarely made on the first attempt; in fact trying to 'close' too early is a sure indication of a lack of professionalism. It takes time to build relationships and research has shown that most B2B sales are consummated after the 5th or more contact between buyer and seller.

As you will see in Section 3, 'closing' in it's more traditional sense should not be the sole focus of a professional B2B sales person in today's selling environment. In fact, 'closing' should be a natural progression of the sales process as it merges with the buyer's journey. But you still need to be 'brave' to engage in a challenging but non-threatening way throughout the sales cycle.

"Victory is sweetest when you've known defeat."
Malcolm Forbes (1919-1990), American entrepreneur and publisher

---

Chapter Two
Knowing What Sales Professionals Know

Right at this moment, there are millions of people out in the world selling something; many are far from being sales professionals enjoying the benefits of a high-rewards career. Perceiving yourself, and conducting yourself as a professional is as important to success as a great attitude.

There's a lot more to being professional than the obvious advice to be well-groomed and well-organised, and to always act with integrity. A sales professional is distinguished from the amateurs by their sheer dedication to their career; and the foundation of operating as a professional is your knowledge.

"He who knows most, knows how little he knows."
Thomas Jefferson (1743—1826),
3rd president of the United States

Over four decades, I have worked with many hundreds of salespeople, and what consistently sets the most successful of them apart is that they know things that their less successful counterparts don't. They take time, and make the effort to develop a strong insight into the markets they are selling into, their prospects and their clients. What they know affects the way they operate as their higher knowing informs a better way of selling by going about creating value for their clients which, in turn, delivers more successful results.

Here are seven things successful salespeople know and act on:

1. They know who their ideal customer is. This might seem obvious and simple, but successful salespeople have this clearly defined and they know this in-depth. They resist the pitfalls of making 'everyone' their customer and drill down to the level of individuals. I recently asked a business owner client of mine to describe his ideal client, and his response was that it is someone "with a pulse and a credit card". He's not alone in making this fundamental mistake; so many inexperienced or unprofessional salespeople aim to sell to everyone. In contrast, good salespeople know that 'less is more'. They identify the specific industries, markets and locations where their ideal customers operate; and they know the areas where they are active. They know the typical challenges they face and the opportunities they are missing—they know which benefits they can deliver to ideal clients that will be regarded as valuable. They are not content to list a company name as an ideal client. Instead they research to understand the key players in their target organizations.

2. They know their product or service, their company and their competition. Again this appears obvious, but good salespeople frame this knowledge from the buyer's perspective. What is it their product or service can do for their customer? What problem does it solve? How does it help increase profits? What value does it add? How does it differ from others in the market? What weaknesses are the competitors likely to target? What are the strengths and weaknesses of the competitors? They are always looking to 'take a walk in the buyer's shoes' which affords them clearer and more meaningful insights.

3. They know how much time to spend on finding the right prospects and customers. Once good salespeople have identified their ideal client, they learn where they 'hang out' offline and online, and they work out how best to communicate with them. Making the right contacts during this process helps them identify the real needs of the organisation and identify those involved in the decision-making process. They ensure that their level of contact and forms of communication are appropriate and purposeful. By following a sound, time-efficient process for finding, contacting and communicating with prospects, good salespeople can detect an unfulfilling prospect early, and more swiftly change course to a pursue a better option.

"Every sale has five basic obstacles: no need, no money, no hurry, no desire, no trust."
Zig Ziglar (1926—2012), American author,
sales guru and motivational speaker

---

4. They know how to build networks. In this information era, research shows that buyers can be 50 to 70% into their decision-making process before engaging with a salesperson. However, further research shows that when a salesperson engages early in the buyer's journey, they have a much greater rate of success.

Good salespeople know that by building their network of individuals and businesses they can learn of opportunities early, as well as gain vital information and insights. By contributing positively and purposefully in a network, they build the credibility of their own personal brand and their company.

5. They know how to develop and sell themselves. Because people buy from people they know, like, trust and respect, successful salespeople know that they have to sell themselves before they sell their company image, product or service. It has become particularly vital for B2B salespeople in the more complex sales arena to know how to develop a compelling personal brand and then to embody it in their offline and online networking, and when they are building relationships with people of influence. As they gain experience and expertise, their personal brands progress towards positioning them as experts in their fields.

So powerful can a personal brand be in today's digital marketplace, I highly recommend investing time and if necessary money in learning how to create the best possible brand for yourself.

"Closing a sale is counter-intuitive. Agree to implement and open a relationship."
Wayne Moloney

---

6. They know how their own system works. All too often, salespeople think their job is done when the order is signed. Good salespeople know that the delivery, implementation and ongoing support of what they have sold are critical to future opportunities. In the interests of maintaining trust in their customer relationships, they take on a certain accountability for ensuring that the organisation's delivery to their customer meets the expectations that they set up during the sales process. To this end, they know that their internal networking is as important as building their external network, and they make the effort to collaborate as a team member across the areas of the business that impact on sales delivery. Good salespeople sell themselves and their opportunities internally as well. They know that senior managers, marketing, support staff, research and development can all have an impact on their ability to deliver what they have sold, on time and in good order.

7. They know when to walk away. Despite doing all the right things in identifying and developing a prospect, all salespeople will, at some time, find themselves working on an opportunity that just doesn't fit the success mould. Good salespeople know that time spent on opportunities that have little chance of success is wasted time. They are able to walk away from a slim possibility to spend their time better on finding or developing the 'right' opportunities.

It may seem that these seven traits come naturally to good salespeople, but all salespeople can improve their success by actively building these knowledge strands and developing a successful way of operating based on the quality of what they know. With knowledge being so important to their sales success, it's not surprising that another common characteristic of successful salespeople is that they are lifelong learners, committed to their professional and personal development.

I use the following questionnaire in my sales training workshops to encourage self-awareness and self-reflection. Take a few moments to quickly provide your answers, on a scale of 0—10 to the 10 statements and note your score.

Do I Think Like a Sales Professional?	Score
1. I am proud and happy to be a salesperson.	
2. I am aware that business conditions are constantly changing and keep abreast of the changes.	
3. I find ways to continually adapt and update my selling techniques.	
4. I make specific efforts to improve my ability to communicate my ideas to prospects and customers.	
5. I have taken courses in salesmanship, public speaking or creative thinking? And/or, have I read more than one book on salesmanship during this past 3 months.	
6. I read books on salesmanship or listen to discussions of selling methods. I look for ideas I can adapt to my own work. I try them.	
7. I study my company's sales material, and use the resources provided as intended.	

8. I try to get everything I can out of sales meetings and contribute as much as I can to the success of those meetings.	
9. I try to increase my success by: a. analysing my own work each month, and b. planning a systematic approach to achieving my goals.	
10. I actively develop my professional personal brand so I am seen as credible and knowledgeable in my target market. (See Chapter 10 in Section 2 to learn how to do this)	
TOTAL	

Rate yourself—Add your answers to get your percentage rating as a sales professional.

How do I rate? _____%

Create an action plan to enhance your sales professionalism

Even if you just scored a 100% rating for your sales professionalism, it makes sense to plan your on-going professional development. If you scored less than 100%, reflect on the strengths and weaknesses you identified in the Introduction exercise to see where you can develop strengths and mitigate weaknesses. Use the template and ideas below to formulate a professional development plan that you can implement.

Sales Professional Development Plan

My Strengths:
1. _____
2. _____
3. _____

My Challenges:
1. _____
2. _____
3. _____

My Development Goals for the next 12 months:

1. _____

2. _____

3. _____

Actions I can take to achieve Development Goal 1:

_____

_____

_____

_____

Actions I can take to achieve Development Goal 2:

_____

_____

_____

_____

Actions I can take to achieve Development Goal 3:

_____

_____

_____

_____

Some ideas of actions that can be taken to achieve sales professional development goals:

Attending formal training—including offline and online courses; presentations, workshops and skills programs that build your positive thinking, self-development, communications, presentation and selling skills

Attending industry-related events—such as workshops, presentations, meetings, conferences and exhibitions to deepen your industry knowledge, keep abreast of changes, increase your visibility and build your personal brand.

Developing a reading (or listening) program—that gets you researching, listing and sourcing the latest and greatest sales and self-development books, and then actually reading or listening to them. If you think that you don't have time for reading, consider how much time you do have during commutes, when listening to the narrations of books is absolutely possible. Some years ago, I switched from reading books to listening to them after I lost sight in my right eye. I was surprised at how much 'learning time' I gained, and really enjoyed, by listening to podcasts and eBooks in the car or on the train. You can also get other members of your sales team to form a sales force book club with you and start conversations about what you've read and learnt. Ask successful sales professionals in your network to recommend books to you. Keep a lifelong list of all the developmental books you have read. You'll find a list of some of my favourites in the Epilogue.

Conducting desktop research—schedule regular time to get on the internet and explore what's out there that can help you achieve your development goals. Listen to podcasts, watch videos and read expert articles that contribute to your self-development, business and industry knowledge

Reviewing your learning—make use of note or journaling software to keep an on-going review of what you are learning. (I use evernote. com at this time, but you might want to keep an eye out for the latest and greatest.) After each intervention, such as attending a course or reading a book reflect on what new knowledge you have gained and how you will use it to do things differently. This helps you to ensure that you implement what you have learnt to get better results, and it also acts as a valuable reservoir of content should you one day want to develop your own expert material.

Engage a mentor—we all need help now and again and gaining insight from someone who's 'been there and done that' can be an enormous benefit. A good mentor should have a strong background in your area of selling, be well connected, be able to challenge and guide you and ask probing questions to help you find your way more effectively. I have been fortunate to have some great mentors throughout my career and even today still work with a mentor to provide me with unbiased support and feedback. Don't be afraid to approach someone—most people are only too happy to assist.

"A mentor helps you envisage the future, and believe it can be achieved."

Chapter Three
Sharpening Your Communications Skills

Much is made about the salesperson's 'gift of the gab'. It is true that good salespeople need to be articulate and confident enough in what they say to be convincing. Strong communication skills are vital. But having your say, however articulate and compelling, is only one aspect of communication. Communication by definition is a two-way process. It is, therefore, only effective when your message is received and understood; and if you listened, received and understood the other person's message in return. Miscommunication happens much more frequently than many of us acknowledge, and it is expensive. It often results in mistakes made and opportunities lost. Miscommunication costs time, goodwill and trust, whether it occurs with prospects and clients or team members and your management.

Communication is not just about what you say. Your verbal message is inseparable from your non-verbal cues such as, the tone and pitch of voice, posture, eye contact, gestures, physical proximity and facial expressions that reinforce or modify your verbal message; define or emphasise your relationship with the other person and convey emotional information. When you communicate you encode these non-verbal cues and the person who receives your message decodes them.

"The single biggest problem in communication is the illusion that it has taken place."
George Bernard Shaw (1856—1950), Irish playwright, critic and socialist

---

Communication can also not be separated from the context in which the message is delivered. Every message is delivered in a particular circumstance which includes the setting and the situation that play a role in giving meaning to the message.

As salesperson on the road to success (or even greater success), you need to have a keen awareness of the actual standards of your communication skills and a focus on developing a real-time consciousness of your communication processes.

Effective communication demands that we:

- are skilled at asking insightful questions
- listen to what others have to say before offering comments or suggestions
- are aware of our own assumptions, viewpoints and feelings
- are aware of the assumptions, viewpoints and feelings of those with whom we are communicating
- are aware of the emotional content of what we are saying
- hear the emotional content of what others are saying
- use jargon sparingly
- regularly evaluate the effectiveness of our communication, both in real-time and as an on-going personal skills audit

- adjust our communication style when necessary so that we communicate at the recipient's level

---

"Our business is infested with idiots who try to impress by using pretentious jargon."
David Ogilvy (1911—1999), British businessman widely acclaimed as the 'Father of Advertising'

Effective listening skills

The ability to listen well is at the core of communicating successfully. It impacts not just on the sending and receiving of messages, it influences the quality of your relationships. We are all aware of when we are being truly listened to, or not, and that plays a key role in building trust.

Effective listening is not just about hearing words someone speaks; it is a dynamic, focused activity that engages all your senses so that you are able to accurately perceive all verbal and nonverbal cues. This is often referred to as 'active listening', a term coined by US psychologist Dr Thomas Gordon.

The levels of listening are commonly defined as:

Level 1—Internal Listening is listening to your inner voice. You may be hearing the words of the other person but are so fixed on what we want to say that we don't pick up on the cues being delivered before we get the chance to have our say.

Level 2—Focused Listening is concentrated listening where all your attention is directed at the other person and what they are saying, to the exclusion of the environment around you. You are purposefully searching for the nuances of the message and actively focusing on 'reading' the client's non-verbal cues. Listening is effective and active.

Level 3—Global Listening is characterised by a heightened awareness that takes in all that the person communicates within the global context of the moment. This includes 'downloading' cues in the environment that will help you better understand the person, their interests and possibly, their concerns. When you listen at this level you are aware of the energy between you and the other person, as well as the energy of place. Your intuition is available to you at this level.

The 5 characteristics of effective listening:

1. **You are prepared to listen**—you pay complete attention to the person with your inner voice shut out. You are content not to speak.

2. **You are paying attention**—you concentrate on receiving all sensory information and process facial expressions, posture, physical movements, breathing, tone, tempo, volume and words.

3. **You are appropriately responsive**—you echo, paraphrase and reflect back to consciously support the flow of communication and ensure the other person is aware that you are listening and understanding.

4. **You clarify and encourage revelation**—you invite disclosure and amplification. You ask for an explanation if you are not sure you are achieving a deep understanding of their message.

5. **You are perfectly patient**—you never interrupt and you allow the other person their pauses by holding the silence.

"Most people think "selling" is the same as "talking". But the most effective salespeople know that listening is the most important part of their job."
Roy Bartell

Effective Questioning

We've discussed in the previous pages the importance of listening, but what you listen to will depend largely on the questions you ask.

For years, sales training was focussed on the difference between 'open' and 'closed' questions. Closed questions being those which can be answered by a simple "yes" or "no," while open questions are those which require more thought and more than a simple one-word answer.

There is a time and place for both types of question. It's a case of asking the right question, at the right time, of the right people, for the right reason. Knowing this can be learned but it is also something that comes naturally to empathetic salespeople looking to understand the business and personal drivers of those engaged in the buying process.

Questioning is all about 'discovery'. When posing questions at any stage of the sales process you should be looking to learn more about the prospect, the opportunity, the 'fit' of your solution, whether there is consensus among those involved in the decision and how value will be defined.

> **"Teaching is not about answering questions but about raising questions…opening doors for them in places that they could not imagine."**
> Yawar Baig

Effective questioning allows you to build rapport and show empathy by developing an understanding of the issues being faced by the prospect. But do NOT ask that clichéd old question "what keeps you awake at night". Your questioning should be such that you are positioned as an 'expert' in your field. Someone the prospect can look to for guidance during their own discovery phase. Your questions should:

- demonstrate what you know about the industry, market and company
- help you understand what you don't know but need to find out to introduce your 'solution' to the business
- determine how important the problem or business improvement issue is to the business and individuals—will they be interested enough to devote the time and effort you need from them, let alone the dollars
- identify how the prospect will define value and can you *really* deliver something that meets this definition
- identify options that will be open to the prospect: DIY, competitors able to deliver the required value, do nothing (accept the status quo)
- help you understand the buying process and where the prospect is on their 'buyer's journey'

An important part of questioning is to be prepared. Know your market. Spend time researching your prospect and the internal contacts online so there is less chance of being surprised and your questions demonstrate the value you can bring to the relationship. No one wants to waste time educating you so you can sell. You need to educate them so they can buy.

Improving communication

Communication has such a major impact on your effectiveness, performance and quality of relationships. It is important for you to regularly reflect on how well you are communicating, and where you can improve. This applies to your contact points with prospects and customer, as well as within your sales team and organization.

Here's a reflection sheet that can be used after an important interaction:

Think back on your engagement with a prospect or client; a team member or management representative.

Did I have a clear objective and did I achieve it? Why/why not?

_____
_____
_____
_____

Where could communication have been enhanced for a better result?

_____
_____
_____
_____

Was I lacking any information that would help make communication more effective?

_____
_____
_____
_____

If I can overcome the communication challenges in this relationship, what results could I expect?

_____
_____
_____
_____

What could I do to improve communication during my next contact point?

_____
_____
_____
_____

The benefits of effective communication

Open and honest communication is a hallmark of a high performance salesperson. If you are trying to boost your results, start with accurately gauging the state of your communications with prospects and clients; and work to improve that first.

There are many benefits of effective communication, including:

Efficient action—when you communicate effectively with a prospect, client or internal stakeholder, you are able to operate efficiently and productively because miscommunication results in lost time and mistakes. Misunderstandings and incorrect actions cause resistance and slow downs, and require time and effort to make corrections and get back on track.

Increased input—when your communication is open and trusted, others feel confident that their opinions, ideas and expertise are welcomed and valued. Key to a successful partnership with a client is for you to harness their talent, knowledge and experience to find solutions, generate new ideas and then guide you internally.

Responsiveness to change—when your communication structure is robust, dynamic and flexible, you are empowered to accurately respond to dynamic changes in the marketplace and your workplace. Effective communication ensures that new and important information is shared efficiently so that you and your prospects and clients are up to speed and empowered to adapt appropriately.

Shared Understanding—when your communication is efficient, it seamlessly brings together diverse backgrounds, perspectives, cultures and experiences that are roadblocks in an inefficient communication system. Focus on achieving understanding with your prospects and clients at each contact point.

Valued relationships—when you communicate effectively, a network of strong relationships is created and maintained. This network of relationships underpins your motivation and performance.

Cultivating your awareness of your communication skills, and actively improving them is an ongoing endeavour for the successful sales professional. Making a habit of reflecting on the communication after each contact point with a prospect or customer will help you to keep your focus on honing this vital skills-set.

"It is not your customer's job to remember you. It is your obligation and responsibility to make sure they don't have the chance to forget you."
Patricia Fripp, American sales trainer and speaker

Chapter Four
Keeping Time on Your Side

There's no doubt that sales is a high pressure career; and most often, the sharpest pressure is related to having enough time to meet our prospecting and selling targets. Although I use the common term 'time management' in this chapter, I actually believe that the phrase is a misnomer. We can't really 'manage' time; time gives us the same 24 hours a day. However, we can use each 24 hour period as the framework for effectively managing ourselves, and this is what I mean by time management.

**"Lack of direction, not lack of time, is the problem.
We all have twenty-four hour days."**
Zig Ziglar (1926—2012), American author,
sales guru and motivational speaker

Many people resist and avoid properly managing themselves. Effective time management does demand a relentless discipline and often requires changing your habits. While this might seem like you have to make sacrifices, the reality is that when you do manage yourself effectively, you actually get more of what you really want, and that should be more than enough motivation for you to keep up the self-discipline.

If you have yet to make a commitment to managing yourself well, or you know that your time management process needs to be improved, I cannot encourage you enough to take action and get time on your side.

Use the following questionnaire to assess how well you are currently managing your time.

Time Management Questionnaire

Using the rating system below, assign your rating to each question:

1—Rarely   2—Sometimes   3—Usually   4—Always

QUESTION	
I prepare daily and weekly to-do lists	
I have a weekly schedule on which I record fixed commitments	
I prioritise the items on my to-do list	
I prioritise my list in order of importance, not urgency	
I spend the majority of my time on the important rather than the trivial matters	
I accomplish the things on my to-do list during the day	
I am able to meet deadlines without rushing at the last minute	
I tackle the difficult or unpleasant tasks without procrastinating	
I set time aside for planning each week	
I find the time I have set aside for planning is sufficient	
I plan time to relax and be with family and friends	

I know when I feel best during the day and time the important tasks for then	
I periodically reassess my activities in relation to my goals	
I delegate tasks that are not necessary for me to do	
I manage my own actions more frequently than I am driven by circumstances or by other people's priorities	
TOTAL	

Total your scores. If you score:

46—60 You have outstanding time management skills.

31—45 You are managing your time fairly well, but sometimes feel overwhelmed.

16—30 You have some time management skills but work is likely to be stressful and less than satisfying.

15 Your time management is poor and your skills are much in need of improvement.

Time management techniques

1. Classifying your tasks

Regardless of what tools you use, time management starts with getting the big picture clear by understanding the relative importance of each task to your overall sales success, and then allocating the appropriate proportion of your time to each task.

To be successful, there are only 3 things a salesperson should be spending their time on each day:

- servicing clients
- working leads and progressing opportunities
- generating new opportunities

Unfortunately we don't live in an ideal world so 'real world' tasks, such as dreaded admin, will need to be addressed as well.

Many productive salespeople classify tasks by type, and then allocate typical percentages of time to spend on them:

- **Type 1 Tasks**—these are the really important activities that are for good business development and keep you focused on current opportunities. Type 1 tasks include planning, making contacts with potential clients, and developing relationships. You need to be proactive about getting these done. They might need up to 60% of your time.

- **Type 2 Tasks**—these cover current ongoing projects and include organising and holding meetings, dealing with incoming calls, and taking reactive action to developing situations. Type 2 tasks need up to 25% of your time.

- **Type 3 Tasks**—these are the routine or maintenance tasks that keep business running smoothly—for example updating databases, dealing with accounts, or writing reports. Type 3 tasks should not take up more than 15% of your time. Today, we have the opportunity to make use of Virtual Assistants that will enable you to cost-effectively outsource many of your Type 3 tasks.

Unfortunately many salespeople let Type 2 and Type 3 tasks dominate their working week. It's easy to let them take up 60% of your time. But this is a stressful way to work and it can also lead to poor sales strategy. Big decisions get rushed through without enough time to figure out all the consequences. New business opportunities can be overlooked.

2. Making daily and weekly to-do lists

Daily and weekly to-do lists are essential tools for managing your activities and the time they take to achieve. They enable you to keep focused on the goals and deadlines that move you towards greater success. It helps to develop a habit for recording your daily and weekly to-do lists by attending to them at the same time each day or going to a particular location where you get them done. Explore, find and use the calendar, note and reminder systems that work best for you. There are numerous apps available that allow you to now carry your to-do list in your pocket.

3. Setting achievable objectives

The first stage in getting a task done depends on setting the final objective.

Make sure you goals are **SMART:**

- **S**pecific—State exactly what you want to achieve? The more specific the description, the greater the chance of success. Ask the '5 W' questions will help—What, When, Where, Why, Who?

- **M**easurable—How will you evaluate and demonstrate the goal has been achieved? Establish specific criteria for determining your progress—benchmarks and milestones

- **A**daptable—this does not suggest your goal should be constantly reviewed and changed when targets are not met, but goals should be able to be refined and focussed as business priorities shift, ensuring the right work is always getting done. (NOTE—traditionally the 'A' in SMART goals refers to Achievable. I believe this is covered by Realistic and in today's fast paced sales world, you need to be able to adapt your goals to changes in your environment)

- **R**ealistic—How does to goal tie into your key responsibilities and objectives? If it doesn't, why is it on your list? Your goal must represent an objective toward which you are both willing and able to work. A goal can be both 'stretching' and realistic; you are the only one who can decide just how high your goal should be and remain realistic. But be sure that every goal represents substantial progress.

- Time Bound—What are the start, finish and milestone dates that will guide you to successful completion?

Having goals, even **SMART** goals, is a waste of time if you don't actually track your progress towards those goals in some way. (I have included in the Epilogue a simple template for building 30, 60 or 90 day work plans to help you achieve your goals.)

4. Effective scheduling

Once you have listed what it is you need to do, you need to develop a schedule that guides your activities and allocates time. Group related items and issues on your list together. Identify your most important activities. Identify the times of day when you operate at your best and schedule your key activities for the day or week during these times. Set time limits for each activity and strive to finish them in the time you have allocated. Develop the habit of preparing tomorrow's schedule at the end of today.

5. Setting priorities

What with prospecting, selling, getting the admin done and dealing with all sorts of issues that arise, it is essential that you are able to determine which activities and issues impact on whether you will meet your goals. Constantly changing your priorities results in a failure to establish a proper framework for getting everything on your to-do list done. Make sure you focus on the important activity not the easy activity.

You also need to learn to differentiate between the urgent and important. Former US President, Dwight D Eisenhower famously said: *"I have two kinds of problems: the urgent and the important. The urgent are not important, and the important are never urgent."*

Now while I may not agree that the important are never urgent, it is true that…

Important activities have outcomes that lead to us achieving our goals, whether these are professional or personal.

Urgent activities demand immediate attention, and are usually associated with achieving someone else's goals. They are often the activities we concentrate on, and they demand attention because the consequences of not dealing with them are immediate.

Use this as your guide to determine the order of your priorities:

- Important and urgent
- Important but not urgent
- Unimportant but urgent
- Unimportant and not urgent (Why is it on your list?)

6. Analysing your time allocation

Make sure your activities are consistent with your goals. Keep a record for how you spend time for one week to analyse what, why and how often you do it. Analyse the trends, identify your 'time wasters' and remove them from your routine. Regularly analyse the tools, processes and systems you use to manage your work and your time to see if they are the most effective methods. Can they become more effective? If so how?

Adopting and adhering to sound sales and business methodologies and processes will help you remain focussed on the activities that are most critical and likely to impact your success. Look for the system that works best for you and start to make it part of the way you engage with your target market.

It maybe that your company has a system that they demand you adopt. If this works for you, great. But if not, I strongly suggest you identify what works for you and determine how this can be integrated into your company's way of working.

Are you a procrastinator?

Everyone procrastinates on occasion but whether procrastination becomes a problem or not depends on how much negative impact it has on your life. Some people put off doing tasks, but finally complete them; yet others cannot ever seem to get a project underway or see it through to the finish. Others confuse procrastination with 'not rushing in'. I have a close friend, a very successful businessman who classed himself as a procrastinator. When we discussed why he thought this it was really because he took time to think things through before acting, considering the risks and potential rewards. This is not procrastinating, it's careful planning.

You can use the following questionnaire to assess whether you are likely to be a procrastinator to the point where it interferes with your effectiveness, and for how well you are using your time.

Using the rating system below, assign a rating to each question:

1—Rarely   2—Sometimes   3—Typically

QUESTION	
I spend time chatting (or on social media) during working hours if I feel under pressure	
I find it hard to concentrate and get focused on a task	
I avoid conflict or unpleasant situations by doing something else	
I complete easier, low priority jobs before the tough tasks	

I spend time worrying about making mistakes before starting on a task	
I miss deadlines because less important tasks have gotten in the way	
I leave difficult tasks to the last minute and complete them under pressure	
I don't clear and reorganise my working area before starting a major task	
I tend to delay implementing plans I have agreed	
I have to make a real effort to get started on a job	
TOTAL	

Total your scores. If you score:

> **24-30 Procrastination is reducing your productivity.**
>
> **17-23 You often put things off and can improve.**
>
> **11-16 You are already aware of procrastination as a time issue but can do more.**
>
> **10 Congratulations, you generally do things when you need to!**

Defeating procrastination

When procrastinating, the best thing you can do is admit it. When you stop rationalising why you aren't doing what you need to do, you're more likely to take the right action. Analyse what causes you to put things off. Most of us tend to avoid things that are unpleasant, complex or overwhelming. You can avoid procrastination by scheduling the toughest jobs first and getting them out of your way. It helps to tackle unpleasant tasks in small pieces over short time segments. If you are avoiding a complex task, break it down into smaller steps, and focus on one step at a time. Sometimes, perfectionism stands in the way of getting things done. Let this go, and take the risk that you may not get a perfect result. Remember: Good enough is good enough! Don't wait for the right mood; make a start in spite of whatever mood you are in.

There are only two rules for achieving anything:

Rule 1: Get started. Rule 2: Keep going.

Commit yourself to action and set deadlines. Promise yourself a reward for completing the task and when you finish, take your reward.

"The way to get started is to quit talking and begin doing."
Walt Disney (1901-1966), American entrepreneur, cartoonist, animator, voice actor, and film producer

---

Plan around your most productive times

We have all heard people describe themselves as 'morning' or 'evening' people, or even 'night-owls'. Karen Leland, a management and marketing consulting specialist, conducted a poll on LinkedIn and found 36% of respondents reported that their most productive time is during the window between 9:00 and 11:00am. Following close behind at 31%, are those who know that their optimal productivity is before 9:00 am. 16% reported that their most productive time is between 4:00 and 6:00 pm. 9% reported between 7:00 and 10:00 pm and 6% reported their peak productivity is between 12:00 and 2:00 pm. It all comes down to knowing yourself. If you know when you are most productive, you can schedule your most critical activities accordingly and this will have a significant impact on your effectiveness.

Work in blocks

Breaking long working sessions into manageable blocks of time and taking breaks in-between will help you remain refreshed and able to continue attacking the task with renewed vigour. Reward yourself when you've met your targets and don't forget to get some exercise. It has been proven time and again that exercise boosts brain function!

Scheduling prospecting

Your time for prospecting must be included in your schedule to ensure that you meet your goals to identify and engage new customers. If you don't really enjoy cold calls, emails to prospects and meetings with them, you are likely to let prospecting fall by the wayside, which will inevitably leave you with an empty pipeline and a sales drought. Prospecting is not something that you do 'when you have the chance'. It is a priority activity for any salesperson and should always appear on your schedule. Taking a structured approach to prospecting can help you to get better results, which would increase your enjoyment of the activity.

In Chapters 9 and 10 of Section 2, I discuss how to use social media properly to minimise the need for old-style prospecting and to engage with prospects in more interesting and fulfilling ways.

Scheduling administrative tasks

If you are like most salespeople you probably hate admin, and would much rather be out selling. However, sales paperwork, and its electronic equivalent, has to be done, and it helps to have a set time in the day to deal with administrative demands and issues. Many salespeople find it easier to schedule administrative tasks at the end of each day, and they take an hour out to keep up with the necessary admin requirements.

The following tips will help you to manage, and avoid being overwhelmed by your administrative tasks:

- There are only four things you can do with any task—dump it, delegate it, do it, or defer it

- Develop criteria for what content you keep and what to throw out

- Can technology help you be more efficient? With the proliferation of available Apps, cloud computing and mobile devices you can streamline your administrative tasks…but you need to choose wisely and ensure you don't create more work for yourself in the process

- Analyse your administrative work to see what can be eliminated, shortened, modified, combined or otherwise improved

- Develop routines, standard responses and templates; streamline everything you can

To manage the top of your desk and computer desktop, ask three questions about every piece of communication that comes your way:

1. Will I really do anything with it?
2. When will I do it?
3. Where will I keep it?

Managing email and social media demands

If you check your email or perhaps your Twitter account every time your phone vibrates, chances are you are often distracted from your tasks at hand. Skipping from unfinished task to unfinished task not only creates stress, it disrupts your schedule and makes it much harder to achieve your goals. Trying to deal with email and social media notifications, as and when they come in, only creates chaos in your day. It helps to have specific times set aside during the day to deal with this. There's no hard-and-fast rule for this. You will have to experiment and find what is most time-efficient for you. Many productive people defer looking at their emails until around lunchtime. Others argue that email should be responded to first thing in the morning and again, early in the afternoon. Some warn that starting your day with email makes you reactive to the wants and demands of others. Explore having a designated slot for email and social media in your working day, and adjust to what works best for you. When it is time for email and other social interaction, have a system for organising what needs to be responded to immediately, what can wait, what can be deleted immediately and what can be quickly forwarded to another to take action.

If you haven't done it yet, making a commitment to effective time management is one of the most critical ways to achieve success in sales, and in life. Using your working hours productively helps to ensure that you achieve a healthy work-life balance and gives you the best chance of reaching your goals.

"A road well begun is the battle half won. The important thing is to make a beginning and get under way."
Soren Kierkegaard (1813—1855),
Danish philosopher and writer

Applying Time Management

Identify one habit you want to change or eliminate:

_____
_____
_____
_____

What is the new habit you would like to develop?

_____
_____

_____

_____

Why it is important to you?

_____

_____

_____

_____

What results do you expect from the change?

_____

_____

_____

_____

Dealing with interruption

Interruptions are part of your job. Keep a record of all your interruptions. Find out who interrupts you, when it happens, how long it lasts, what it was about. Look for patterns. Allow enough time for interruptions in your daily schedule. Keep interruptions short and focused. Bunch things together and handle several things in one visit or call. Try standing up when someone comes into your office, or when you answer the phone. Standing up is a better position for controlling how long the interruption lasts.

You may implement some time management processes and techniques and experience some improvements in your productivity and performance. However, I urge you not to leave it at that. Keep reflecting on your processes; keep looking out for new ways to be more efficient and focused, and keep abreast of the latest advice on time management. Practice different techniques, try out different tools and whenever necessary, adopt different habits that will better support your success.

Chapter Five
Taking Charge of Yourself

No matter what position you may occupy in an organisational hierarchy, you are still the leader and manager of your own life. One of the reasons most of us choose a career in sales is because of the freedom it offers. Freedoms go hand in hand with responsibilities, and therefore, we need to be our own boss—a leader and manager.

Taking on the attitude that you are a leader in everything that you do will ensure that you are operating with the mindset required to constantly create success in your life. You become an effective leader by demonstrating leadership qualities whenever they are required by any given situation. You make a commitment to the high performance expected of leaders across the domains of self, home, work and community.

> **"Accept responsibility for your life. Know that it is you who will get you where you want to go, no one else."**
> Les Brown (1945—~), American motivational speaker, author, radio DJ, former television host, and former politician

By the nature of the profession, salespeople operate with a great amount of autonomy. So, it's no surprise that good sales professionals are self-directed and accountable individuals who take full responsibility for the activities required to meet their targets. While for some, these characteristics may come naturally; others actively work at developing their leadership qualities.

Apart from having the capacity to effectively manage your own performance, another important reason to focus on your leadership abilities, is that you frequently need to demonstrate the qualities of a leader and take on leadership roles when you act as a customer's trusted and valued advisor and effective solutions provider or challenge their status quo to make them think of the unexpected.

Leadership roles—What is it that effective leaders actually do?

1. **They set the goals—success is not left to chance**; strategically define and plan what you want to achieve across all areas of your business and personal life. Always know exactly what it is you are working towards whether that's a monthly sales target, a specific sale, a career milestone, an intimate change of attitude or a family holiday of a lifetime.

2. **They innovate—there's always room for improvement**; be constantly on the lookout for new and better ways to support you in achieving your goals. Avoid resting on your laurels, and instead restlessly search for innovations and create opportunities that can help you to enhance your performance.

3. **They solve the problems —there's no such place as 'stuck'**; find the ways to move past, around or through difficulties, hindrances, barriers and setbacks. Never accept that you have an insurmountable problem in your way. Be absolutely determined to find the solutions that make things possible.

4. **They make the decisions—someone has to**; take charge of your performance, your career and your life by being constantly willing to decide on the next course of action. Of course, decision-making means risk, and maybe every decision you take won't actually be the best one. Make decisions anyway.

5. **They define the priorities—what to do?** Everyone's resources are limited and it is up to you to decide how best to deploy yours. You can become adept at knowing what to choose over others if you are absolutely clear about what you want to achieve and understand its relative importance to your goal.

6. **They influence others—teaching at 'the school of example'**; set the tone for your interactions with others by your character, attitudes, habits and the way you treat them. If you are steady, impeccable and empathetic, as though everyone is watching you 24/7, you will make influential impressions.

7. **They deliver results—it's the bottom-line**; don't accept less than what you aim for. Keep your goals top-of-mind; have a single-minded focus on results and do not be waylaid by excuses and stories that justify not delivering the intended result. Make a commitment to always deliver to the very best of your ability.

Review the 7 roles of a leader above and then reflect on your performance at work, in community and in regard to yourself. Use the table below to record examples of where you are playing leadership roles in your life:

Leadership roles	At work	In my community	For developing myself
The last time I set a goal was when I….			
The last time I introduced an innovation was when I…			
The last time I solved a problem was when I…			
The last time I made a significant decision was when I…			
The last time I defined the priorities was when I…			
The last time I positively influenced others was when I…			
The last time I delivered great results was when I…			

Now review your reflections on your involvement in leadership roles by answering the following questions:

1. Is there an area of my life where I play all 7 leadership roles? Do I find this easy or hard? Why?

2. Is there an area of my life where I don't play many leadership roles? Why? How could I find more opportunities to play leadership roles in that area of my life?

3. Are their particular leadership roles that I find easy or think I am good at? Why? Can I leverage these strengths in any other area of my life?

4. Are their particular leadership roles that I find hard, or that I avoid, or that I think I am not so good at? Why? How can I develop more confidence and capacity to play these roles more frequently and successfully?

Leadership qualities—What are effective leaders actually like?

There's a great volume of research and writing on leadership characteristics and qualities. It is not my aim here to attempt to give you any sort of definitive theory of what makes a great leader. I hope to cue you into the importance of developing your leadership capacity, to gain some insights that you can act on and to encourage you to make an ongoing exploration of leadership part of your personal and professional development.

Leadership qualities come to light in your relationship to self and your interactions with others; as well as in your choices and your outcomes. It is not uncommon for many of us to comfortably demonstrate our leadership qualities in some aspects of our lives, but not in others; or in relationship to some people, but not to all. It can help you to reflect across all important areas of life—not just work, but in community, in family and in the private relationship you have with yourself. The goal would be that you are playing leadership roles and showing leadership qualities with great consistency in your life as a whole. By reflecting holistically, you can better leverage your strengths and mitigate your weaknesses, as you gain greater understanding of yourself, how you operate and how you are perceived by others.

Use the following 'Highlighting Leadership Qualities' tool by getting a green highlight pen and highlighting each and every quality that you think you demonstrate in a mostly consistent way, or a red highlight to show where you think you could improve

Highlighting Leadership Qualities

You can more than double the value of this tool by giving it to others who experience you in leadership roles. Ask them for their candid responses and then compare their feedback with your self-assessment. Deeply consider any anomalies between your perception of yourself and theirs; because this can lead to your greatest growth as a leader.

The following tool will help you to gauge your leadership skills. Consider all areas of your life, not just your role at work. You can also look at this from a position of thought leadership, not simply people leadership. In today's sales environment, being recognised as a thought leader in your field can deliver significant opportunity and provide opportunities for engagement that will not come to those who sit and wait for things to happen:

Leadership Self-Assessment

Using the rating system below, assign your rating to each statement:

1—Rarely   2—Sometimes   3—Usually   4—Always

QUESTION	SCORE
I reflect on my personal values and principles, and I understand how they impact on my behaviour and also have an effect on others	
I actively ask for feedback from others, and adapt my behaviour when necessary	
No matter what the task at hand, I am committed to consistently deliver at the highest standards	
I am calm and focused under pressure	
I seek out opportunities to learn and develop, and actively apply what I learn	
I am open and honest; inclusive and respectful of diversity	
I look for ways to collaborate; and I encourage the contributions of others	
I share ideas, information and resources	
I listen to others; and take their points of view, feelings and needs into account	

I plan for success, evaluate performance throughout a process and make adaptations when necessary	
I speak out when I notice that ethics are being compromised	
I communicate clearly and effectively	
I keep my word	
I take the necessary action when resources are not being used effectively and efficiently	
I put forward new ideas and solutions	
I am aware of the current drivers of change, and see what adaptations need to be made	
I anticipate future challenges	
I can articulate the need for change and influence others to adapt	
I analyse information, including the feedback I get from others, to find ways to improve performance	
I acknowledge and appreciate others	
I make decisions when they need to be made	
I take responsibility for my performance	
I am excited by opportunities for improvement	
I acknowledge my mistakes	
I seek opportunities to play a leadership role	
TOTAL	

Total your scores. If you score:

76—100 You have excellent leadership skills and should optimise on all opportunities to take on leadership roles to build your profile as a leader.

51—75 You have clear leadership potential, but need to be more focused and consistent. Actively look for more opportunities to be a leader and hone your skills

26—50 You have some leadership skill, but need to develop your leadership qualities as a priority. Consciously apply leadership qualities in all areas of your life so that you start to develop the habits of a leader

25 Your capacity for leadership is underdeveloped and this should be a key focus area for self-improvement. Actively learn more about leadership. There are many great resources available. Research leaders you admire such as historical figures, outstanding entrepreneurs and the captains/managers of your favourite sports teams. Analyse what qualities contributed to their success, learn from their experiences and apply what you learn in your day to day life.

In summary, review the last two exercises and complete below:

My top leadership strengths are:

1. _____
2. _____
3. _____

Right now, I could use these strengths to:

1. _____
2. _____
3. _____

My top leadership challenges are:

1. _____
2. _____
3. _____

Right now, I could address these challenges by:

1. _____

2. _____

3. _____

There is probably no other profession quite like sales to offer more opportunities for you to develop effective self-management habits that will enable you to operate at the highest level of performance. Being the leader of your own life empowers you to achieve the success you really want to see in your life.

Chapter Six
Committing Yourself to Teamwork

The sales profession is one of the most competitive fields in life; and not surprisingly, top salespeople are often very keen competitors. This, combined with the high degree of independence demanded by the job, can result in a lack of understanding of the benefits that can be achieved through teamwork.

**"If you want to go fast, go alone.
If you want to go far, go together."**
African proverb

Whether you're a small business owner with few staff or a member of a sales department, a driving force behind your successful performance is the team with whom you share a common mission and the business objectives of your company. In most organisations salespeople operate in teams, led by a sales manager (captain of the team). Sales teams can also have 'teams within the team' combining, for example pre-and post-sales support or to address a particular opportunity. Sales professionals have to pay as much attention to the need to be a collaborative and effective team player, as they do to being an individual performer. After all, it doesn't mean much to be the superstar of a mediocre or a struggling team. You have a vested interest in doing whatever needs to be done, even if that is more than you are asked to do, to give yourself the opportunity to be at the top of a team of winners. Outside of my work environment my greatest passion is sport. I have been involved in many different sports, participating as a player, coach and spectator. One thing I have found consistently in my many years of involvement with sport is that a champion team will beat a team of champions. And that in a great team each player 'grows' on the back of the others success, they are prepared to back-up each other and they are willing to help each other grow and develop. The end result being a win-win situation for the individual and the team.

A good sales team is one that finds the majority of the team members having positive attitudes, willing to support and to challenge others on the team and hold each other accountable. The team, as a whole, is driven to be successful. A real good team only feels success if all the members of the team are successful. This doesn't mean a team with a weak or struggling member isn't a fantastic team, just that the team itself won't ever feel they are at their best until all members are succeeding at high levels.

Good sales team are also well-trained teams and have a positive attitude when it comes to attending team meetings and training.

When it comes to the individual team members, good sales teams are filled with professionals who simply make other members better. Think of any great professional athlete that makes the others on his or her team perform better and, as a result, the entire team is more successful.

The same is true with sales teams. No one on a team wants to be the weakest link and be the cause of the team missing their goals. Inspired by this, a good team is filled with professionals who strive to improve. This focus to not being the weak link puts positive pressure on other team members and drives others to improve.

In all my years in sales and sales management, I have witnessed all types of sales personalities, styles and cultures. Often salespeople are 'lone wolves', going it alone and focussing on their personal goals and objectives. While I have seen many successful sales people of this style, those that enjoy the greatest long-term success are those who have worked as part of a team including the client and their own support team.

Loyalty is rewarded with loyalty

An effective team player demonstrates many fine qualities, but one of the most important is surely, their loyalty. Cultivating a strong allegiance to your company, your team, your other colleagues and your clients is an important aspect of your development as a sales professional, and it lays the foundation for success in sales.

We make choices about where to place our loyalty, and find reasons to justify why someone or some entity doesn't deserve our loyalty. It might well be that loyalty is one of your strong personal values, and that you pride yourself on always 'having the backs' of your family and friends; team members, colleagues and clients. However, many of us may find it easy to demonstrate loyalty in particular areas of our life, but have to work a bit harder to cultivate our loyalty in the workplace.

Take a moment to reflect on your degree of loyalty in the workplace, and give yourself a rating, where a score of 0 is having no feeling of loyalty and 10 indicates a fierce and consistent faithfulness that is reflected in your thoughts, words and deeds:

I am committed to my company 0 ——————— 5 ——————— 10

I am committed to my team 0 ——————— 5——————— 10

I am committed to my other colleagues 0 ——————— 5 ——————— 10

I am committed to my clients 0 ——————— 5 ——————— 10

If you scored less than 7 for any of the above, reflect on the reasons why and write them down in longhand on a piece of loose note paper. Read over your list of reasons not to give your loyalty. How quickly and easily did the reasons come to mind? Now, crumple up that piece of paper and put it in the recycling as a symbol of making a new start, and here's the reason why:

The benefits of loyalty to:

Company—*your loyalty to your company demonstrates that you believe in it.* It may not be the 'perfect' company; it may not currently be an industry leader, but it is the company you now represent—and if you don't believe in your company, its products and services, then you have little chance of transferring that belief to a prospective customer. You greatly increase your chances of gaining and retaining customers by being committed to your company. It is important to note that loyalty doesn't equal 'turning a blind eye'. A loyal salesperson will help the company or team become better, by constructively highlighting weaknesses that need to be addressed and so playing a role in business and team development.

Team—*your loyalty to your team members underpins your relationships with them and demonstrates that you belong.* A strong commitment to each other and the team, as a whole, lays the foundation for the effective teamwork that is required to achieve shared objectives. Caring for how the team operates and performs is rooted in feeling loyal.

Colleague—*your loyalty to other colleagues builds the wider network of relationships that you need to be successful.* There is a developing trend at this time that demands that salespeople be more engaged in the value chain of the business, and particularly more directly involved and aligned with the marketing department in order to deliver value to customers in a highly competitive environment.

Clients—*your loyalty to your clients is essential if you are to be a trusted advisor to them.* Loyalty has become one of the most sought after qualities of our time—everybody wants 'hard-to-win and hard-to-keep' customer loyalty. Well, loyalty is rewarded with loyalty; and if you want your client to turn to you as their trusted and valued advisor again and again, over the long term, then offer them your loyalty first. This will also see prospects and clients willing to engage with you when you endeavour to challenge the status quo of their business.

8 Characteristics of an effective team player

Demonstrating high-level qualities such as loyalty makes a major impact on your effectiveness within a team, as does expressing certain behaviours. Like leadership, teamwork and team dynamics have been widely studied. Here are some of the main characteristics of a valued team member:

1. **Completely reliable**—You can always be counted on to keep your word, meet deadlines, get tasks done, deliver quality work and make your targets. Being consistently dependable, not just sometimes, helps the team to keep on track and fosters positive relationships with team members.

2. **Communicates effectively**—You communicate clearly and honestly while respecting the views, opinions and ideas of all other team members. You listen actively to others and give them thoughtful consideration, even when you don't agree with them. By focusing on candid communication you

help the team avoid the miscommunications that hinder relationships and derails performance.

3. **Shares information**—You are generous when it comes to sharing your ideas, knowledge, sources and opinions with the aim of supporting other team members, boosting team performance and strengthening bonds. By not assuming that others know what you know, you offer suggestions and propose solutions that help to bridge information gaps and give other team members an advantage. The popular saying: 'Knowledge is power', attributed to English philosopher, Sir Francis Bacon, has for a long time been taken literally with people wanting power keeping knowledge to themselves. In today's online world, power comes from your ability to be seen as an expert in your field, which is a complete about-turn. Today, power comes from sharing knowledge and creatively developing and applying insight from that knowledge.

4. **Avoids politics and resolves conflict**—Without making judgements, you steer clear of the gossip, bad-mouthing and power-posturing that can harm relationships within the team and the company. You deal with conflict quickly and maturely by following a resolution process that does not 'blame and shame' the other person. You don't let yourself get distracted by issues that aren't critical to the team's goals and help to keep the focus on what's really important for everyone's success.

5. **Adapts quickly**—You don't fuss, complain or stress when situations change, but find your feet quickly and easily so that you maintain focus on the goals. With a flexible approach and a 'can-do' attitude, you help others to not just tolerate, but optimise disruption.

6. **Values others**—You recognise that others have different work styles, different qualities and different contributions to make. You appreciate this diversity and are aware that it brings resilience, innovation and dynamic balance to the team. You acknowledge the benefits to you of the assistance, inputs and support you receive from others.

7. **Gives others the benefit of the doubt**—When you perceive a team member as irksome or troublesome, you don't assume that it is something to do with you and speculate on their underlying motivations in a way that casts them in a villainous light. By avoiding the perceptions of comments, looks or inattention as personal slights, affronts and snubs, you are able to maintain peaceful and positive relationships that strengthen the team.

8. **Shows real commitment**—Your commitment to your team is obvious. You see your contribution to the team as much more than just making your individual targets. You make the effort to prioritise having positive relationships with your team members. You readily provide support when others need it or ask for it, even if that means doing more than what is expected of you, or more than others do.

"It is amazing what you can accomplish if you do not care who gets the credit."
Harry Truman (1884—1972), 33rd President of the United States.

The benefits of effective teamwork

Teamwork is a proven, reliable method for getting high quality results from the efforts of committed people. Teams can provide a synergistic return on investment—when the whole is greater than the sum of the contributing parts, then 2 + 2 will be greater than 4. The other benefits of teamwork include better outcomes, ideas and solutions; the improvement of business efficiencies and competitiveness; and the creation of an environment where team members experience mutual support, encouragement and a heightened sense of accomplishment. For the highly individual salesperson, team success helps the business grow, which in turn makes the brand more valuable resulting in an easier sales cycle delivering greater rewards to the individual, the team and the company.

The characteristics of an effective team

Most members of high performance teams report that it's fun and satisfying to work on collaborative teams because they are asked to contribute at their highest potential and they learn a lot along the way. Characteristics of high performance teams include:

- people have solid and deep trust in each other and in the team's purpose—they feel free to express feelings and ideas
- everybody is working toward the same goals
- team members are clear on how to work together and how to accomplish tasks
- team members share leadership as they support, mentor and coach each other
- everyone understands both team and individual performance goals and knows what is expected
- there is a clarity of role for each team member
- each team member carries their own weight and respects the team processes and other members
- team leadership adjusts to meet the needs of the individual, the team and environmental shifts to drive results.
- no individual members are more important than the team

Some common roadblocks to effective teamwork

Just as a chain is as strong as its weakest link, so a team is as effective as its most ineffective member. A single problem member will have a dangerous effect on the strength of the entire team. Poor teamwork quickly becomes exhausting and demoralizing.

Here are some of the most usual issues that arise in teams. Each team member should have both a right and a responsibility to raise the 'red flag' and recommend a resolution if they experience any of these roadblocks:

1. Proceeding without a plan

Working according to a plan is not just the responsibility of the salesperson, but of the manager and the manager's manager. It starts at the top with the Board or business owner having a clear vision that is passed down to the next level, who in turn set their own objectives.

The following have to be clearly defined, communicated, known and understood by all team members:

- Goals
- Plans
- Challenges
- Actions
- Timing

If you as a team member don't have a clear understanding of this, it must be addressed with the team leadership.

2. Incomplete or flawed team processes

Team processes are how the team goes about what they need to do to achieve their goals. High performance teams thrive on well-designed, thorough processes that map out the step-by-step actions that must be followed to achieve results.

The following are indicators of incomplete or flawed team processes:

- Too little participation
- Too much participation

- Over-talking/failing to listen
- Ridicule/stereotyping
- Poor time management
- Lots of activity but little accomplishment
- Strained relationships
- Miscommunications
- Low productivity
- Poor results

3. Unsound decision-making process

Whether it's by design and agreement, or just an organic development, every team follows a process when it comes to decision-making. This decision-making process makes a critical impact on whether or not the team is going to be effective. Indicators of an unsound decision-making process are:

- conflict avoidance—effective teams benefit from sharing their points of difference
- early agreement—ineffective teams feel the need to establish a common view quickly
- voting/averaging—leads to poorer decisions and is more likely to lead to dissatisfaction
- win/lose—It is not always possible to have a win/win scenario, but when one party wins at the 'expense' of the other, conflict and resentment result. Good teams manage these situations through open discussion.
- suppression of minority views—robs the team of the richness of diversity

4. Settling for second rate

Struggling teams may not want to face the realities of their situation, and instead tacitly settle for low performance. The indicators of this are:

- low commitment
- indecision
- compromising
- guarded communications
- conflicts without resolutions
- personal criticism
- running out of time
- avoidance of reality testing

A model for effective teamwork

Many of the common problems of teamwork can be avoided by operating in accordance with a teamwork model that supports high performance.

Teamwork is a repetitive cycle of planning, controlling, reviewing, learning and planning again:

PLAN—Why are we here?

- What are the team's and each member's individual goals?
- What are the team and individual game plans?

CONTROL—How are we doing?

- Setting and watching milestones
- What tasks have or have not been achieved?

- Are team members working as a team or a group?

- Are we meeting our deadlines?

REVIEW—What have we achieved?

- Performance against goals and targets

- What do we need to change?

If you think that your team members or leadership group would benefit from the information in this chapter, then make sure you share it with them. By communicating your expectation to be part of a high performance team, you can provide direction and inspiration that can raise the bar for everyone.

"Remember, teamwork begins by building trust. And the only way to do that is to overcome our need for invulnerability."
Patrick Lencioni (1965—~), American writer

If you find yourself on a good sales team, you will be supported and driven towards getting better at your position and will likely have a greatly increased chance of success. However, just being on a good sales team does not guarantee your success and cannot replace good, old fashioned work. You still need to constantly work at improving your sales skills, attend as much training as you can manage in your busy schedule, seek out a good mentor and battle against the daily grind to keep your motivation levels high.

If you find yourself on a bad sales team, your greatest challenge will be not allowing the bad team to hurt your motivation for success. Ultimately, you are responsible for yourself and while others on your team may not be supportive or helpful, you are still in charge of your future.

Chapter Seven
Planning for Your Success

In all my years of business mentoring probably the greatest challenge I experience is getting salespeople to invest the proper time and effort in planning. Some argue that living in the moment and acting on inspiration when it strikes is most likely to win them the sales success that they want. In my experience, I certainly haven't seen a lot of that happening! By contrast, I have seen plenty of successful salespeople diligently and regularly applying themselves to the planning process. That doesn't mean that your plan has to rule your life. Your plans should be your guide, and when things that you didn't expect turn up, you need to be flexible and adjust accordingly.

"You have brains in your head. You have feet in your shoes. You can steer yourself any direction you choose."
Theodor (Dr Seuss) Geisel (1904—1991);
American writer and illustrator

So, what is planning?

1. Planning is the thinking process that we go through before taking action to achieve an objective. Planning involves deciding what to do about the most probable course of events within a range at possibilities.

2. The development of objectives and the determination of the means by which these objectives are maintained.

3. Deciding in the present what to do in the future.

The benefits of planning

Some people wait for the future to happen. They may well have goals, especially in the form of dreams, but they drift through life in the present, hoping something different may just turn up on their horizon someday. Others are driven to literally craft their way into the future that they want, and they do this according to a plan.

Having a plan helps you to:

- focus your attention on objectives
- improve your efficiency
- offset uncertainty
- be prepared for change
- monitor and control your activities

> **"The nicest thing about not planning is that failure comes as a complete surprise and is not preceded by a period of worry and depression."**
> *John Preston, Boston College, Graduate School of Management*

Your Plan is a Roadmap

If you don't plan, how do you know where to go? You wouldn't jump into your car with the intention of driving from A to an unknown

B without a GPS, a map or at least, directions. You may get there eventually, if you're lucky, but how long will it take?

The planning process helps you to clarify and articulate where you want to go. It leads you to identifying the best route. In essence, your plan is a roadmap to get you on the right road to success. Planning is preparation, and being well-prepared gives you the confidence that you will get to where you want to be, as well as a valuable measure to ensure that you don't lose your way.

The characteristics of a good plan are:

- **It articulates goals**—your objectives are expressed clearly and concisely.

- **It specifies actions**—when you decide on the actions you will take to achieve your goal, you set events into motion and identify the steps you need to take to close the gap between your current reality and the future you want.

- **It provides a time-frame**—a specific timetable drives the momentum of a plan. Next to nothing ever gets done 'sooner or later'. Every action needs to be executed by a certain time

- **It will be flexible**—you cannot anticipate everything the future holds, so your plan must be a 'living' document that allows for contingencies and adapts smartly when necessary.

The importance of goal-setting

The beauty of formulating a plan is that it all starts with defining our objectives. One of the most common traits of successful people is that they set goals, they write them down, they plan how they will achieve them and carry out their plans. You can use goal-setting in any area of your life where you want to see change, development and progress. The process of setting your goals enables you to clarify what you really want and need in your personal life and career. It also helps you to break a seemingly impossible, monumental aspiration down into rolling hills that you can navigate progressively. As you set goals and achieve according to your plans you develop vital confidence in your ability to 'make things happen' for yourself, instead of being buffeted by 'things happening' to you.

Sales Forecasting

Successful salespeople develop forecasts and/or sales budgets. These are effectively a projection of achievable sales revenue and provide the basis of an organisation's business plan because the level of sales revenue affects practically every aspect of a business. Forecasts are based on historical sales data, analysis of market surveys and trends, and salespersons' estimates.

Any sales planning must start with a forecast.

If sales forecasting is not part of your company's sales procedures, it is most likely that you will be expected to contribute to sales forecasting, and if not, you need to be forecasting your own sales for your own benefit. The level of granularity of your sales forecast will vary depending on the nature of the products or services you are selling. As a minimum, your sales forecast should provide a month-by-month projection of the volume of sales that are expected over a specific period of time, usually a year. The sales forecast serves the business as a whole in many ways. The sales forecast will influence budgeting throughout the business and will help to establish the levels of activity for other departments. For example, in a product-focused company it is vital to determine how much to produce, what kinds of products should be made, and how many people will be necessary to produce or distribute these products.

The sales forecast is used by a business to assist in:

- determining the quantities of skilled people, raw materials and supplies the company needs to buy to make the products or provision services

- defining the production schedule for the products
- planning and schedule people resources
- making an inventory of finished products
- deciding on the best product or skilled resources mix
- guiding the marketing and advertising efforts
- estimating the number of salespeople needed to sell the products or services

By their very nature, sales forecasts will never be 100% accurate. Unforeseen changes in the market, the economy and your own business will impact your forecast, however you should strive to provide a realistic estimate of the revenue you will be able to generate. To come up with a sales forecast that is as accurate as possible, you will need to take the following into consideration:

- the last year's month-by-month actual sales per customer
- the current pricing and the market price indicators
- your competitors' activities
- other market indicators and trends
- general economic indicators, current and anticipated

It stands to reason that the more accurate your sales forecast is, the more useful a tool it is for you and your company. A wildly inaccurate sales forecast will have direct detrimental impact on a company's efficiencies, cash flow and profitability. This is why it is important to review and assess the sales forecast on a regular basis in order to make strategic modifications.

Businesses that have accurate sales forecasting processes may enjoy benefits, such as:

- understanding when and how much to buy
- the ability to accurately plan for production and capacity

- in-depth knowledge of customers, their buying profiles and patterns
- the ability to identify and respond quickly to sales and market trends
- an indication of the worth of their business above the value of its current assets
- the ability to determine the expected return on investment
- improved cash flow and enhanced profitability

The following table is a simple example that shows you how to use the sales forecast on a month-by-month basis to assess the contribution of existing clients and determine the value that needs to come from new business. It can be used for both products and services. This report is intentionally oversimplified and does not replace what you may be using in your company's CRM; it is provided to show that forecasting does not need to be complicated—Keep It Simple.

HOW TO ANALYZE LAST YEAR'S SALES

Last Year's Sales Month: January		This Year's Projection Month: January	
Customer	**Amount**	**Customer**	**Amount**
Dynamo Ind.	$ 4,250	Dynamo Ind.	$ 4,000
Abbott Prod.	$ 1,300		
City Purchasing	$ 3,725		
Swan Farms	$ 2,696	Swan Farms	$ 3,500
Nepean Parts	$ 5,284	Nepean Parts	$ 5,000
Stern Manufacturing	$ 4,008	Stern Manufacturing	$ 5,200
Offset Press	$ 2,425		
Studio supply	$ 813		
Donald & Sons	$ 1,866	Donald & Sons	$ 2,300
Putty Inc.	$ 3,525	Putty Inc.	$ 3,000
		Hockey Co.*	$ 1,500
Actual Sales Last January	**$ 29,892**	**Projected Sales from Existing Customer**	**$ 24,500**

This year's January target	**$ 32,500**
Anticipated orders from existing customers	**$ 24,500**
	———
Gap that must be filled by new business in January	**$ 8,000**

*Hockey company is an existing customer who did not order last January, but is expected to place an order this January.

As mentioned above, this example is intentionally oversimplified, but is typical of the first pass of sales forecasting I have used successfully throughout my career. Once this high-level projection is completed, you should break it down by month and product/ service type (see Territory and Pipeline Planning, page 102).

Projecting Sales in the Services Sector

When selling in a service-based business, sales forecasting can be tricky. Companies which are providers of services face the additional challenge of the erosion of existing business, for various, often unplanned, reasons.

- How much existing business is safe?
- How much is at risk?
- How much business development is necessary?

The following diagram shows how your entry level revenue will be eroded over time as clients leave (this is referred to as 'churn') and your base price is eroded. An example of this is evident in the mobile phone market where prices are continually dropping and clients frequently change service providers.

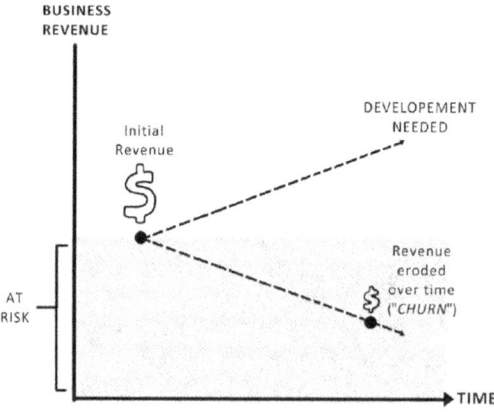

Both business-at-risk and business development must be planned for. Some questions to reflect on are:

- How will you best protect your client base to minimise erosion?
- How will you generate new revenue?
- Where will it come from?

What new products or services are in the pipeline for which you might need to plan?

The Planned Step

I am a firm believer in keeping things simple. Whether you need to develop a sales plan, your call plans or a sales plan for a product set or a territory—they should be short, sharp and to the point. Before starting to map out your plan, consider your priorities. Decide what you need to focus on:

- Short term sales
- Longer term position for larger opportunities
- Generating referrals
- Generating recurring revenue
- Providing the company and yourself with *identity*

"The future will depend on what we do in the present."
Mahatma Gandhi (1869—1948); Indian activist

Here is a straightforward 5-step framework that enables you to develop a short and simple, strategic and tactical sales plan.

As you work through this process, don't just *think* about your answers…this does not create action. *Write* your answers down. For some people this is enough to keep them accountable. If you find sharing your goals helps you keep accountable and motivated, do so; but make sure you are sharing with someone who will provide positive encouragement and support, not a naysayer. Welcome this accountability so you remember and continually move towards your goals for the year. If you have chosen to work with a mentor, share with them and get their input in developing your forecast.

Now, let's take a look at each step of the roadmap.

Step 1—Goals

Confucius said "A journey of a thousand miles starts with one step". Your first step is to know where you want to go.

Start by considering in what key areas you should set objectives. This might be revenue retention, new business generation, focus on specific markets, the number of clients, product/service mix, size of average order etc.

Understand, define and agree on SMART objectives that we discussed in Chapter 4:

- Specific—What exactly do you want to achieve? The more specific the description, the greater the chance of success. Setting a goal of reaching your $1.2million target is not specific. Setting a goal of achieving $100,000/month is more specific, but could still be improved. Asking the '5 W' questions will help—What, When, Where, Why, Who?

- Measurable—establish specific criteria for determining your progress—benchmarks and milestones

- Adaptable—our goals should be able to be refined and refocused as business priorities shift, ensuring the right work is always getting done.

- Realistic—Your goals must represent an objective toward which you are both *willing* and *able* to work. A goal can be both 'stretching' and realistic; you are the only one who can decide just how high your goal should be and remain realistic. But be sure that every goal represents substantial progress.

- Time-based—a goal without a deadline is not a goal. Deadlines are what make most people switch into action. So install realistic deadlines and go after them.

Step 2—Planning

When you know your goals, it is time to plan how to reach them. Plans are important because it breaks goals into manageable pieces and forces you to think about the specific actions to achieve them— the strategic initiatives and tactics you will employ. It also makes you check-in on your goals to ensure progress is being made.

The first task in this step is to conduct an audit of 'where you are now and how you got there'. Think about where you want to be— your goals. Think of the pieces that will make up the goal.

Ask and answer these questions:

- What is my current position?
- How are my sales results?
- What markets am I addressing?
- Who are my current clients?
- How did I get to where I am today?

Many plans fall short at this point as salespeople fail to thoroughly understand their current position and they fail to consider both the big picture (territory) and the finer detail (pipeline)

Territory Planning

Planning should start with an analysis of your territory. The 'area' assigned to you from which you will generate your sales. Depending on the processes adopted by your company and management, this may vary from one organisation, sales team or individual salesperson. It may be defined by geography, demography, industry type, product/service or a combination of these.

Next, segment your known clients and prospects; identifying current clients and known prospects and determining the opportunities that exist within each. This will give you a base of 'known potential revenue'. Simply deducting this from your target will allow you to determine the gap you need to fill with new business.

The following questions will help you on the above:

- What are the key trends in your geography/market?
- Who are your top prospects and customers?
- What are customers buying?
- Based on your conversion rates, how much business do you need in your pipeline?
- What is the gap between what you need in your funnel and what you have now?

At this stage of your planning you should have a thorough understanding of why your clients buy; consider:

- What are the characteristics of your high-value clients?
- Are there specific industries or sectors of industries (vertical markets) where you and/or your company is more successful than others? Why?
- What value can you deliver to your clients? Pain solved and/or business gain?

- What compelling events drive purchases?
- Are there specific products/services that you are selling more than others? Why?
- Why do prospects not buy your products/services?

Before creating an action plan (Step 3), you should consider the strategies and resources you will adopt and require to achieve your goals:

- Which vertical markets or geographies will you focus on?
- Where do you need to improve your sales process?
- How will you further penetrate current clients?
- Who inside the typical client can help? How can you build a relationship with them?
- What internal and external resources can support your efforts?

'Pipeline' Planning

A sales pipeline is a measure of all opportunities segmented by the level of development in the sales process. (see Section 3)

Over time you will develop an understanding of the likelihood and time required to move an opportunity through each stage of the sales cycle and of course, the probability of success will increase as your prospect moves through your pipeline. This will allow you to place a 'weighting' (percentage of likely success) against each opportunity which in turn will help you understand the additional opportunities needed to reach your target (see Section 3, Stage 2)

Step 3—Determine actions needed for success

I find a simple way of making a plan is to 'backcast'. I think of having achieved the goal and then work backwards to define what

I needed to do to get there. Now you need to be very specific. What needs to be done and when?

- Document what you know
- Document what you should know but don't
- Acquire missing information

In a 'simple' sales environment you may look at now using averages to help understand the required activity needed to build and manage your pipeline. If your company has kept good records, you will be able to establish the average success ratio of proposals to sales. Then it may be possible to extrapolate from historical sales records, the number of phone calls needed to get an appointment, and the number of appointments required to submit a proposal. Although this is based on averages, and of course, will vary from one individual to the next, this system does work, particularly in transactional sales environments.

A client of mine in the building industry has over 30 years of sales history on file and he knows that for every 100 enquiries he receives, his sales team can organise 75 initial meetings. From these meetings they can generate 40 proposals and receive 5 contracts. When sales start to fade he checks the trends and 9 times out of 10 it is because these ratios have slipped.

Yes, this is a B2C example, but for non solutions-based and more transactional sales, this simple, tried and tested method still works. Understand the steps that are in your sales cycle plus the average success rates for each step and then calculate what numbers you need to make at each step to hit your target. From here you can start to plan the actions necessary for success.

A critical step in determining your actions is knowing your competition. Evaluate the competition in each segment and likely to be targeting the your client and prospects. Gather data on these organisations that repeatedly compete for business in your sales area. Buyers are going to make their decision to buy (or not buy) based on the alternatives they have. If you know what the alternatives are, you are in a better positioned to compete.

Step 4—Identify Challenges

Laying out a plan will quickly make clear challenges that must be overcome and the risks that may negatively impact your progress. Thinking ahead about potential risks and challenges will prepare you to bypass, or address these and move towards your goal.

Think ahead of the potential challenges to your proposed plan. Then, identify the quickest ways to solve these challenges or the best action to take if these challenges become a reality.

"Plan for the worst and hope for the best" is a motto worth considering in putting together your sales roadmap.

Step 5—Create a Timeframe

When are you going to start?

The biggest barrier to success is not starting. At this point, you will be setting yourself target dates to achieve specific actions that you have identified to achieve your goals and objectives.

If you create a timeline, you have to get it done. You need to tell yourself and your collaborators (manager, family, staff, partners) when things will be completed.

Create quarterly check-in points and break your goals into the shortest time periods possible to work in sprints instead of marathons. Have a set of key performance indicators (KPIs) that will help you stay focused and identify negative trends that might impact you reaching your goal.

If you reflect on this framework and happen to feel some resistance to actually going through the planning process, then remember this…**"By failing to prepare, you are preparing to fail." Benjamin Franklin**

A well-conceived, clear plan based on honest and accurate assessment, is one of the greatest advantages you can give yourself. Success rests on a plan.

Call Planning

It is essential that every call you make on a customer creates value for the customer and if possible progresses an opportunity. If you do not create value for the customer the customer is less likely to give you more time; and time is the most valuable asset your prospect can share

---

Time is the most valuable thing a man can spend.
Theophrastus (ca. 371—c. 287 BC), Greek Philosopher

Planning your daily activities goes a long way to helping you achieve your sales targets. An overall call plan establishes your calling pattern, however, you should also be planning each and every call that you make. All too often, salespeople do not have a clear objective for the calls they make. Particularly in face-to-face sales engagements, the salesperson has to ensure that each sales call has maximum effect for themselves and the client. As the qualification process advances, the salesperson has to ensure that each client engagement is optimally successful.

To this end, there is a need for the call planner that defines:

- What is my objective on this call?
- What questions do I need to ask?

- What information—particularly valuable and unique commercial insight—do I need to convey to deliver value to the prospective customer?
- Where is the prospect on the Buyer's Journey?
- What is needed to continue progressing the sale?
- Is it time to assess if the prospective customer is ready to commit?

Success in sales will come from delivering value that is recognised and appreciated by your client, reducing waste in your sales process, measuring your risk and minimising it on each engagement.

Time to plan

As part of your time management system, it is important to schedule your time to plan. This includes not only the time it takes for you to formulate a new plan, but a regular, weekly check-in on existing plans where you review your goals, the actions completed and those ahead. Reflect on the relevance of your goals through time, adapt your plans when necessary and don't forget to celebrate achieving milestones.

Section 2
Understanding Relationship Selling

Over many decades the question of "How to sell successfully?" has been answered with an ever-evolving array of sales methodologies and solutions, approaches and processes. This evolution has succeeded in dragging selling out of the manipulative dark-ages.

> **"Real integrity is doing the right thing, knowing that nobody's going to know whether you did it or not."**
> Oprah Winfrey (1954—~), American media proprietor, talk-show host, actress, producer, and philanthropist

While some of these sales processes of the past have naturally become out-dated and would be considered inappropriate today; some have aspects that are still relevant when adapted to our current sales environment. In essence, it was not so much the particular steps in any methodology necessarily becoming irrelevant; as it was about the manipulative approach of older selling styles becoming an unacceptable way to engage with customers.

In the 1950's, the B2B corporate world was focused on Transactional Selling that involved the 5 'AIDCA' steps—Attention, Interest, Desire, Conviction, Action. The 1960's saw the emergence of Tactical Selling focusing on Feature, Function, Advantage, Benefit. Over time, we saw a mellowing of aggression in the sales approach. Sales people started to align with the customer to build rapport and develop trust—this, to me, was the real start of relationship selling. The 1980's introduced Solutions Selling that resulted in sales people engaging at higher levels than they did in the past. At this time sales people looked to identify where the political power lay and to understand the problems and opportunities the prospect faced so that they could deliver a solution. From a sales perspective the focus was making sure you put time and energy into the right places and right people by asking the right questions.

We are now moving into an era of 'Value-based' Selling and 'Insight' selling when relationships are more important than ever as buyers and sellers align even more closely, and the buyer's journey interweaves with the sales cycle; and the line between sales and marketing becomes more blurred. The salesperson's role is to fully understand the buyer's business, their needs and budget; and go further by even providing ideas and insights that will deliver gain or address pain.

	Product Selling	Solution Selling	Insight Selling
Type of Dialogue	Feature Function Benefit	Exploring Needs	Influencing change
Sales Person Orientation	Product	Customer Solution	Change Agent
Customer Interface	Procurer	Coach/ Advocate	Strategic Change Leader
Dialog Starts When?	Customer specifications (Late)	Customer defined needs (Mid)	Customer is learning (Early)
Information flow	Customer driven (RFQ)	Customer guides buying process (RFP)	We influence buying process
Value Focus	Lowest Price	Differentiated Value	Game Changer Value

Source note—thanks to John Smibert, Custell Pty. Ltd. for use of this graphic

There are still many methodologies used, such as SPIN Selling, Target Account Selling, SNAP Selling and Challenger Sales that all define the 'how to make sales' by instructing on qualifying, managing and strategizing opportunities. They all rely on the same thing—building trusted relationships with the prospects. As

I mention in the Introduction, when I talk about 'relationships' in this book, I am not referring to the more recent perception of sales relationships. Building relationships *does not* mean striving to meet every demand and need of your prospect or customer. It is about developing a *'relationship of trust'* based on empathy; showing you understand their market and business, offering insight into how they can address business issues and challenging the way they currently do business.

In the previous section, I have encouraged you to actively explore, read and develop yourself as a sales professional. If you act on that, there will be no doubt that you are often going to come across the 'latest and greatest' trends on how to make sales. Some of these may offer ideas and insights that do contribute to your development; and some may deepen your understanding of sales practice. It is up to you to consider whether you are being promised a fast and easy track to success at the expense of others or whether the advice will help you to genuinely develop as a sales professional who adds value to others and enjoys enduring success.

Like every other aspect of life, the sales environment is always changing and the savvy professional will always be adapting to new ideas, new market forces and new technologies. If someone had told me 20 years ago, that today I would be paying attention to presenting my professional profile through an internet channel like LinkedIn I wouldn't have believed them. But, here I am, really enjoying the engagement opportunities that today's technology affords me. The reason for this is because I can see how these changes present the opportunities I have always appreciated— the openings to develop relationships with people to whom I can deliver great value, again and again.

The effective development of strong, productive relationships all comes down to our deep, internal intent. If our primary driver is an intent to help others—to give, to create value, to lead others to outcomes that benefit them—then we will behave accordingly. Our behaviour will lead to trust. Trust will lead to action. A customer's action influenced by our leadership in many cases will lead to reciprocal value for us through an order. But the closing of that order must not be our primary intent because our resulting behaviour will not elicit trust. Otherwise we will be seen as focused on our own selfish needs and not those of the customer, and the relationship will not develop.

"No one likes to feel that he or she is being sold something or told to do a thing. We much prefer to feel that we are buying of our own accord or acting on our own ideas. We like to be consulted about our wishes, our wants, our thoughts"
Dale Carnegie (1888—1955), American writer, lecturer and developer of self-improvement and sales training courses

---

Chapter Eight

Tried and Tested Relationship Selling

The roots of relationship selling can be traced back to the late 1960's in an approach called 'needs satisfaction selling' that advocated that through the process of a sale, the salesperson should uncover the needs of the customer and show how their product and service could meet those needs. Over time, that basic concept has evolved into what we now call consultative or relationship selling.

> **"The way you position yourself at the beginning of a relationship has profound impact on where you end up"**
> Ron Karr (1956—~), American speaker,
> marketing consultant and author

What is relationship selling?

Regardless of whether you adopt a solutions-based or value-based approach, or whether you follow Target Account or Challenger

Sales methods, relationships are critical to your success. Relationship selling turns the traditional transactional approach, based on selling a product with certain features, on its head. It is rooted in establishing genuine rapport with clients, placing an authentic importance on the client's best interests and building trust. The focus is a sales process that involves creating a comfortable relationship with your prospect, finding out their needs and delivering something that meets this need, presenting them with opportunities to address unseen challenges or achieve business gains they may not of considered. You're essentially providing a solution that delivers *real value* to the customer, rather than selling a product or service. In relationship selling, you take the long view. Rather than foist a product on a hapless prospect in a moment so that you meet an immediate target, you aim to enhance the lifetime value of clients by being a valued advisor who they turn to regularly, boosting your targets over the long-term.

This approach has two great benefits:

- **for you and the client**—it means taking much of the pressure and discomfort out of the selling process;
- **for the business**—it means developing a long term relationship with clients that will really improve their lifetime value—and that can be worth many hundreds of times the value of any individual sale. The laws of reciprocity will help ensure that your needs are looked after.

How does relationship selling work?

Relationship selling is based on understanding the prospect or client's needs—their business needs, personal needs and their 'hot buttons'. But to develop a relationship so that the client feels safe and confident to reveal themselves to you, you also have to make the effort to understand the human being behind the title 'client' or 'prospect'. No two buyers are alike, and you need knowledge about personality types, as well as the sensitivity, flexibility and dexterity to easily accommodate people's individuality. You develop relationships with prospects during the stages of the sales cycle, so that as their needs are revealed you are able to present your solution to meet their needs—all in a seamless process where the transaction is simply a natural next step.

Are you fit to build relationships that are both personal and professional?

As you can see, making a success of the relationship selling approach hinges on your own capacity to forge and sustain trusted relationships. Some people are naturally charismatic; they find it particularly easy to get others to engage with them and they encounter little resistance as they enter into relationships. However much charisma helps at the onset of a relationship, it still has to be backed up with something more substantial for those relationships to be enduring.

Remember that people buy from people they know, like, trust and respect.

Prospects won't buy anything from you if they think you're insincere, experience you as a time-waster or most importantly cannot see that you can add any value to their business. So while you interact with them, you need to make it easy for them to genuinely like you.

Here are a couple of tips:

- **Feel positive**—emotional energy is contagious. If you are honestly enthusiastic; pleased with where you are, who you are with and what you are doing in the moment, chances are it will engage and uplift the prospect. However, note that faking enthusiasm won't work. It's your energy that is important, not your act. If you find that you are simulating enthusiasm, you need to work on developing a positive attitude so that you can be truly enthusiastic.

- **Give them all your attention**—focus completely on your prospect or client. Be fully present to them. Actively listen to them. Put them first in the encounter, and let go any thoughts about yourself and your performance, your pressures and your needs. The time to focus on you comes after an interaction when you reflect on how you did. When the prospect or client is in front of you, they are all that is happening.

- **Be friendly**—If you are going to make assumptions, as we are easily prone to do, then assume the best of your prospect. Engaging in a spirit of acceptance, with a curiosity to know more about a person, is a foundation of being sociable, pleasant, approachable and likeable. Make the offer of alliance and friendship, at first on a professional basis, and be open to letting the relationship develop on a more personal basis.

- **Practice 'honesty is the best policy'**—You would hardly be human if you haven't experienced at some time, bending or side-stepping truth because you felt pressured, intimidated or threatened. Salespeople need to be vigilant in ensuring that these kind of survival-level motivators do not trigger any dishonesty on their part in a customer interaction. Would you buy from someone you didn't trust? No, you wouldn't. Stick to the truth.

- **Ask questions**—Questions are so important in social interactions and relationship-building. It is a win-win situation where you express your interest in another person while finding out more about who they are, how they think and what they need—information you really need to know. Take a genuine interest in knowing the person before you. Actively listen to your prospect's story as it unfolds, and keep asking questions.

- **Be mindful that your prospect's time is precious to them**—Today, everyone feels extraordinary time pressure. If you want busy prospects to take your calls, agree to meetings with you and give you their time, you need to make very sure that you are relevant to them. Get to the point at the outset and stay on point.

- **Be prepared to 'challenge' the status quo**—as you develop the relationship you should be looking to challenge the decisions and directions taken by your client. This, of course, is not done in a superior or authoritarian manner, but to be the trusted and valued advisor you cannot be a 'yes person'.

   A client of mine recently provided a referral for me and suggested one of the key benefits I delivered to the business was "He's not afraid to have the tough conversations where needed to provide a wake-up call, or offer warts and all feedback"

- **Know your stuff**—this does not simply mean to know the technology of your business, but you must know the business of your technology. How will your product or service impact the customer's business? Become an expert in your market.

"The only way on earth to influence other people is to talk about what they want and show them how to get it"
Dale Carnegie (1888—1955), American writer, lecturer and developer of self-improvement and sales training courses

---

Understanding different personalities

People are different and therefore their motivations to buy differ. It would also be rare for a prospect to change their behavioural style to suit a seller. A salesperson on the road to success needs to understand that, and be aware of the individual they are dealing with. Understanding the buyer's personality and being able to adapt our own behaviour to optimize the connection helps in building strong relationships. This does not mean being manipulative, dishonest or untrue to yourself. It is about demonstrating acceptance, building trust and opening up the pathway to mutual respect.

While it is not fool-proof when it comes to the detail of the individual, which is where the salesperson operates, the classification of personality types does help in broad strokes to provide a guide as to the perceptions, thinking and actions of people. Further, as decisions are increasingly made by committees, understanding the personalities of each person in the process and knowing how to help the committee reach consensus can be extremely valuable in positioning yourself and your proposed business offering.

Analysing personality types dates back to the Ancient Greeks who identified 4 distinct personality types—choleric, sanguine, phlegmatic and melancholic. This has long been further developed, and sometimes, complicated beyond usefulness. In my training of salespeople, I convey the gist of an enduring personality analysis in a fun, but still accurate way, by relating personality types to animals.

If there is any one secret of success, it lies in the ability to get the other person's point of view and see things from that person's angle as well as from your own.
Henry Ford (1863—1947), American industrialist and founder of Ford Motor Co.

Bear in mind, that while we will have a propensity towards a prevailing personality type, most of us are blends. Analyse and assess the characteristics you can identify in your prospect. Tailor your manner and communications accordingly so that you accurately reflect your understanding of them.

Use the following table to assess the personality makeup of a prospect. Don't look for a clear match and absolutes; you could get surprised when a monkey roars. You'll get more value from this tool by identifying and weighting the different aspects to form a more accurate personality profile of a prospect or client. While you are at it, add to your personal development by identifying your own personality profile:

Creature Comforts	Behavioural Style	Behavioural Style Insights
LION Focuses on Controlling the Environment 	• Challenge • Authority • Opportunity for advancement • Fast results • Freedom from control • Efficiency of operation	**Goals** • Getting results • Doing it and doing it now • Being in charge • New opportunities and challenges • Opportunity for advancement • Initiating change and taking risks • Wide scope of operations **Fears/Avoids** • Being taken advantage of • Losing control over the environment • Boredom • Being tied to routine • Appearing weak or soft **To be More Effective** • Develop more patience with other people • Learn to negotiate with others • Develop greater awareness of other people's needs • Participate more with others

When selling to a Lion, you need to be efficient, effective and focus on results. Don't waste time, over-socialise, make assumptions or emphasize that which is unnecessary or they may see as trivial.

Creature Comforts	Behavioural Style	Behavioural Style Insights
MONKEY Focuses energies on influencing or persuading others 	• Popularity • A positive warm environment • Public recognition • Approval • Meaningful Rewards • To work with people	**Goals** • Being involved with people • Having fun while getting things done • Helping people talk things out • Freedom from responsibility for following through on details **Fears/Avoids** • Being blamed for things going wrong • Having people be upset with them • Not being liked or accepted • Public humiliation **To be More Effective** • Be more effective in making decisions • Develop more organised, systematic approaches to tasks • Improve follow-through by attending to key details • Learn to be direct and firm in confrontation • More control over use of time

Monkeys are energetic so you need to match this with your approach. Show enthusiasm for them, their business and their project. Monkeys will want to socialize so you have to get to know them personally and let them know you. Don't be over-technical, create work for them or be unclear with decisions.

Creature Comforts	Behavioural Style	Behavioural Style Insights
DOG Focuses on co-operating with others to carry out the task 	• To keep the status quo • Harmonious relationships • Consistent procedures • Sincere appreciation • Recognition for service • Establish group effort	**Goals** • Being involved with people • Everyone doing his/her share • Things running smoothly • Stability and security • Conflict-free environment **Fears/Avoids** • Situations where nobody knows what is happening • Confusion and instability • Lack of clarity on expectations • Interpersonal aggression **To be more Effective** • Learn to handle change better • Become more assertive • Increase comfort with open conflict • Vary routines occasionally • Become receptive to short-cut methods • Increase verbalisation of thoughts and feelings

Dogs are faithful if treated well and get the attention they deserve. Don't fail to follow up or meet your commitments. Always show consideration for the client, their business and your interest in a long-term relationship. Be patient and 'nurture' them through changes.

Creature Comforts	Behavioural Style	Behavioural Style Insights
OWL Focuses on what is "right" or correct way to ensure quality and accuracy	• A formal environment • Quality standards • Evidence to support claims • Clear performance expectations • Personal autonomy • Accuracy and details	**Goals** • Specific criteria for performance • Accuracy • Setting and meeting high standards • Opportunities to analyse and assess • Logical, systematic approaches to work **Fears/Avoids** • Unwarranted or personal criticism • Criticism of their work • Changes and surprises that may affect performance • Spontaneous displays of feelings • Environments that require personal disclosure **To be more Effective** • Develop more comfort with emotionally charged situations • Learn to value informal interactions with others • Adjust standards to the needs of the environment • Practise confronting directly rather than through indirect means.

If you are selling to an Owl, you need to ensure you are providing evidence of your quality and capabilities. You need to answer questions accurately and take a logical approach to the engagement.

Do not appear disorganised, be over-social or have gaps in the knowledge you are expected to have. And do not rush things.

Getting in front of the prospect

Before engaging with a prospect, remind yourself of the basic rule of selling:

Sell *yourself* before you sell a product or service.

Why?

Because people buy *you* before they buy your product or service, and in today's market, *how you sell* is often more important that *what you sell*

The internet and social media have changed the buyer's journey, the way buyers engage with sellers. Much research indicates that by the time a prospect agrees to engage with you they have usually got more information on your company and your product or service than you could imagine. They also may have come across your personal brand online. But there is emerging evidence that in high-value, more complex B2B sales, where the salesperson is engaged with a prospect during their 'Awareness' stage they are up to 90% more likely to win the business than those engaging later in the buyer's journey.

This results in two important aspects to 'selling of yourself'. The first is that you have to have a professional, well-developed online profile that helps you to sell yourself before this engagement happens. The second is that by the time you engage with the prospect, you need to start selling yourself right away.

How do you do this in three steps?

- **Believe in yourself**
- **Believe in your product**
- **Believe in your company**

In this order! You can't sell something you don't believe in; so if making a sale means the customer has to buy each of these, YOU must first BELIEVE in each of them.

It is important to keep in mind that interacting with a prospect is not about you. It's about the customer and what you, your company and your service can do for them—the *value* you can deliver. Take a walk in the customer's shoes to understand what issues they are facing and what your service can do to ease their pain or create and improve their opportunities.

Stay open to truly understanding what your customers need and what they think they want. If you try to sell people *what you think they need*, you will almost always fail. If you **find out what they want** and **package it with what they need**, you will almost always succeed. Giving customers what they want is an important part of developing your relationship. It will make you a trusted advisor and more than just a salesperson.

In setting out to build relationships with your ideal clients, ask yourself these simple questions:

1. Will they see me and my product or service as relevant to their needs?

2. Will they see me/my company as someone who can provide value?

3. Do they see, or are they likely to see value from our relationship?
   - a problem I can address? or
   - the potential of the opportunity I am presenting?

4. Will they see me as someone who understands their industry, market and business?

5. Will they see me/my company as someone they can trust?

If you can't answer these questions you will struggle to build a relationship. Start early in your interactions with prospects to find the answers. If you discover that the answers are negative, then this is not your ideal client and you should walk away before using up any more of their and your time.

"You can close more business in two months by becoming interested in other people than you can in two years by trying to get people interested in you"
Dale Carnegie (1888—1955), American writer, lecturer and developer of self-improvement and sales training courses

---

Bringing value to your relationships

Throughout my sales career I enjoyed strong relationships with the clients who made me most successful. I was not always the most technically adept in the fields in which I was selling, but I always took the time to understand what I could deliver to the client's business— where I could truly add value. To this end, I became a trusted advisor.

In consulting, I have worked with businesses to develop similar sales cultures.

One client built a strong relationship with the General Manager of one of their most profitable clients. This was both a personal and business relationship. While buying decisions were always based on the value that was delivered, my client was able to develop a level of trust whereby his account manager was 'consulted' when any new offers were received or changes to their environment were suggested to his client. The client would ask questions of him such as: Did they see these offerings as relevant to their business? Could they offer competitive alternatives?

Without a strong personal and business relationship, this would just not be possible.

You become a valued advisor by:

- knowing and understanding your ideal clients' business issues and needs

- introducing relevant commercial insight that is of specific value to the client

- demonstrating that you can offer solutions to their problems, and address their needs

- being proactive in presenting opportunities to the business that may prevent problems or create opportunities

- keeping it simple—communicating at the client's level and making it easy for them to understand what you can do for them.

- being accessible—not at the 'beck and call' of your clients, but showing them that you want to be part of their team, you are keen to help and share their pain.

- maintaining communication by becoming an invaluable source of relevant information, trends and other market information. The key word here is 'relevant', you don't want to overwhelm a busy client. Subscribe to quality newsletters and blogs that speak to your client's business. Look for articles that would be of interest to them and share. Consider spending the first 30 minutes of your day reviewing your subscriptions and forwarding items of interest to your clients.

- sharing contacts—if you are able to pass on contacts to your clients that will help them build their own networks in a positive way, you are adding value. Who is in your LinkedIn network or contact list who can mutually benefit from an introduction to your client?

- knowing when to say 'no'. If you cannot deliver the best solution to a client's problem, say so. Nothing builds trust better than walking away when you can't be the best.

Chapter Nine
Relationship Selling and Social Media

"The modern business professionals are ***digitally*** *driven*,
socially *connected* and ***mobile*** *empowered*.
We need to adapt to be relevant."
Jill Rowley, Social Selling Evangelist

We are operating in the fastest-changing technology and communications environment ever known and it makes on-going, significant impacts on how we go about our business in sales—from finding prospects, to sharing information that builds rapport and nurturing relationships with existing clients. While you may not be a 'tech-geek', you need to be aware of what is happening in your market; how your clients and prospects are getting their information and making their decisions, what communication and social media channels they prefer—and then, you need to get involved.

Used effectively, social media can make business research and lead generation quicker and more efficient, helping to improve a salesperson's productivity. However, the poor use of technology will have the opposite effect, and the power of social media to be distracting needs to be properly considered. You need to use your time most effectively and efficiently, and technology can help with this.

"Sellers who've embraced social media are creating new opportunities that totally bypass traditional sales channels…It's about good selling—using all the tools that are available to you today."
Jill Konrath, American sales strategist, speaker and author

How social media can support relationship selling

Regardless of the changes in technology and how we do business, relationships in selling are still needed for your success. Due to social media, relationship selling has different aspects nowadays, but is very much alive. People still buy from people they know, like, trust and respect, and who can help them be successful. This applies at all levels of selling.

I was recently working with a client who provides training to individuals, corporates and government. One of the sales reps had noticed that even individuals that were buying the training courses were checking both her own and the company's LinkedIn profiles before making a decision to purchase.

Being known is an important aspect of today's professional sales cycle. With prospects potentially being as far as 60 to 70% into their buying cycle before they actively engage with potential suppliers, your challenge is to become known, liked and trusted in the internet and social media environment.

The buzzword for finding, connecting with and relating to prospects and clients through social media channels is 'social selling'. Channels such as LinkedIn, Twitter and Facebook regularly build and launch tools to enable businesses to engage via social media in ever-evolving ways. There's no point in making any recommendations about channels or tools in this book because the rate of innovation is simply too fast. You have to be scanning the social media environment, talking to people about what they use, searching for updates and reading the 'how to for business' guides on the key platforms on a continual basis. What you do need to understand is where 'social selling' can help you in your sales process. Tools are available to help you 'listen' to the market and specific businesses, manage and publish and track your content, provide buyer insights and prospecting; just to name a few. Mapping out what you want to achieve and then using the right tools to achieve this is important and enlisting support to help you with this aspect of your selling can have a significant positive impact on your results.

It is also very important to understand where your ideal client 'hangs out' online. For instance, the training company client I have just mentioned knows *their* ideal prospects in the construction industry are not engaging with social media, but those in other industries are (NOTE—this does not suggest that other roles in the construction industry are not engaging on LinkedIn. In fact my recent findings are there is considerable buy-in from this industry). Recent research in Australia has suggested that more than 60% of the owners of small and medium enterprises are not active on LinkedIn, but they do use Facebook. (They would probably use LinkedIn to check your credentials, though.) So it's horses for courses, and understanding social media is not just about generating leads, but building your profile and credibility in the relevant online spaces.

Understand that all selling is social; relationship-based—that hasn't changed. Social media simply provides different channels for what potential buyers have always done—they still ask for advice from friends, voice opinions, share their pleasure at what has worked for them and deliver forceful commentary when products or services disappoint or fail them. Now they commonly use social media to more widely get advice, share 'over the garden fence' and indulge in angry letter-writing in the form of comments and posts. The beauty of this change for salespeople is that what used to be strictly private is now accessible to you, your competitors and the world; and this radically opens up your field for connection, engagement, understanding—and sales.

It is essential you monitor and respond appropriately to commentary on social media. Disgruntled employees, unethical competitors and clients who may feel they have received less than expected from your relationship can all anonymously post to review sites with negative views.

A client of mine recently had a situation where an online review site had anonymous postings that were quite scathing of the service received. Knowing my client as well as I did I knew these had to be untrue. It took significant time and effort to prove them to be false and while unable to have them removed from the site, it is now obvious from the significant, certified positive reviews that these e questionable.

Why change to include social selling?

Recent research is highlighting compelling reasons for salespeople to embrace change, define their social selling strategies and get online to engage.

Consider these findings:

- a 2012 Aberdeen Group research brief reported that salespeople who use social media professionally are 79% more likely to achieve their quotas than those who don't

- a 2013 Aberdeen Group research brief found that salespeople who include social selling in their activities outperformed their counterparts who don't by 73%, and they also exceeded their quotas 23% more often

- A 2016 Hubspot infographic reports 61% of organisations engaged in social selling report a positive impact on revenue growth

- A 2015 Aberdeen Group research brief found users of social enablement content average 69% more revenue growth year-to-year compared to their peers

- 63.4% of social sellers report an increase in their companies sales revenue compared to those not engaged in social selling (MHI Research Institute, Social Selling Update for 2015)

- Social sellers realise 66% greater quota attainment than those using traditional prospecting methods (How To Make Your Numbers, SBI 7th Annual Research Project, Sales Benchmark Index)

But, perhaps the most compelling reason is that social media is just where more and more of the customers are, and it is how they increasingly want to interact. All the major social networks are growing at the rate of millions and millions of users each year. The salesperson who doesn't use social selling risks being left on the side-line, completely missing out on the game that's growing in status and scope online. And according to an IDC 2014 report, buyers who use social media have larger budgets—typically 84% larger than the budgets of buyers who do not use social.

"It takes 20 years to build a reputation and five minutes to ruin it. If you think about that, you'll do things differently."
Warren Buffett (1930—); American businessman and philanthropist

---

Here are 5 ways that you can use social media to be more effective:

1. **Being in the right place at the right time to meet the sales opportunity**—participate in the forums and groups that involve your prospects and clients by offering insightful comments, posting relevant questions and sharing useful, quality content. By doing this, they can earn trust over time and continually encourage engagement. Take the long view of social media and patiently build your reputation and deepen connections.

2. **Gathering market intelligence from social media interaction**—it takes a focused approach, such as establishing a social selling pipeline that's aimed at gathering and interpreting data to optimise on the wide range of information that is posted, liked, shared and commented on across social media channels. A regular presence in the groups and forums where your prospects are can result in building up significant profiles of prospects you are yet to meet. You will be privy to many of their interests, views, opinions, complaints, likes and dislikes, as well as the real-time events and experiences they are going through. Another key opportunity is to learn about your customer and any issues or challenges they have by listening to *their* customers on social media. Social media offers all these same benefits in monitoring your competitors.

3. **Getting in front of a buyer in a different way**—there's no doubt about it, social media can help you identify prospects more accurately, quickly and easily. Many people are far more open and articulate about their intentions and their problems that need solutions than they ever were. They provide an assortment of real-time signals by asking advice from followers on Twitter, liking and sharing on Facebook, commenting on forums and posting their status on LinkedIn. You can now understand prospects' needs better as they unfold in real time. Further, by monitoring the market and

what other businesses are doing, you can identify 'triggers' that may present opportunities for you to approach clients and prospects with opportunities to challenge the way they currently do business.

4. **Leveraging social media networks**—not every worthwhile connection has to be a prospect. Take note of your contacts' social media networks and focus on engagement that can result in them providing referrals and connections to prospects who are hard to reach in off-line environments.

5. **Managing your social media interaction to get results**— take strategic action across your social media profiles based on the market intelligence you have gathered. Reading the signals highlights opportunities you can act on—for instance:

   - a person's complaints about one of your competitor's products or services may indicate a current receptivity to your business

   - on-going positive exchanges with a prospect on a particular topic may be a sign it's a good time to share more significant content or even have a conversation in person.

   - the personal likes or dislikes of a prospect might serve as a useful ice-breaker when you do decide to make contact outside of the channel

The information you gather via social media should be treated and used with care. Avoid making assumptions, test out your hunches and make light, professional approaches.

Measuring the impact

As with any other sales strategies, you need to track your time and activities across social media channels so that you see results; gauge their effectiveness; get advice if necessary; monitor progress and recognise successes. There are hard deliverables that you can measure over a time period, such as the numbers of:

- decision-making prospects that have been identified
- social media contacts converted into personal contacts
- sales derived from social media contacts

Social media rules of professional engagement

Like other technologies, social media is a tool that you can either use to great effect or cause damage. You need to follow a clear, well-defined code of conduct that governs your social media activity. Here are some insights to guide you:

- **Maintain the focus on the buyer's agenda**—The Number 1 rule is NEVER, EVER sell on social media. Yes, you can put offers on company websites and sell there, but not on your personal profiles. I immediately disconnect from anyone when they send me an invitation to connect and then follow up with what they can do for me or what great offer they have. 'Social selling' is really a misnomer, it's really 'social marketing' or 'social engagement'. Social media prospects are no more of a captive audience online as they are off-line. Salespeople's whose posts and comments come across as pushing their sales agenda can expect to be effectively blocked and their online reputations will be more vulnerable. The content you share must maintain the focus on solving problems, adding value and helping to achieve the prospect's objectives.

"Social is not a place for a hard sell—it's a place to build trust and credibility. Work the intelligence into your formal sales process and messaging while staying top of mind by continuing to interact on a personal level over social media."
Julio Viskovich, Canadian thought-leader on social selling and digital marketing

---

- **Give to get**—There was a time when the person who had the knowledge had the power. These days the power lies with the person who shares the knowledge and related insight. As part of developing yourself in today's world of social media, you need to embrace the concept of 'give to get' by actively sharing content that is relevant, interesting and empowering to others and relying on the laws of reciprocity. Giving to get not only warms up your connections, but it plays an important role in building your personal brand.

> **"Knowledge is power"**…Francis Bacon, 1597
> **"Sharing knowledge makes
> one valuable!"**…Wayne Moloney, 2017

- **Share, but beware of over-sharing**—You should share your personal branding information, as well as your professional views, news, opinions, comments and updates. Be cautious about sharing personal information, avoid sharing inappropriate content and be aware of sharing information in such a way that it makes one appear weak, foolish, irresponsible, unreliable, unintelligent, immature, biased or over-zealous. Content should always be shared in a context that makes sense for the receiver. Content in context is likely to be of value to your customer

- **Maintaining privacy in public**—Be vigilant about using the full privacy settings on those social media sites that you maintain for your personal connections, and on those profiles connect only with people you actually know as friends. Be aware that it is essentially impossible to be anonymous and confidential when it comes to the internet. It is wiser to anticipate that the content you share, even in the guise of usernames; as well as content about you that is shared by others, is most likely to follow you. It can be useful to clean up personal social media sites by deleting posts and updates, and un-tagging yourself from photos that others have shared if this content presents you in an unfavourable light.

Manners are even more important—it is vital to engage professionally across social media, to avoid controversies and show more restraint than you would in face-to-face interactions. It is much harder to correct misunderstandings, to rectify mistakes and to gauge whether an apology or an attempt to reconcile has actually worked in the online environment.

Social selling is no longer something the professional B2B salesperson can ignore. 'Social' is a critical and integral part of a salesperson's toolkit. It needs to be understood and utilised.

Chapter Ten

Your Personal Brand

Creating a social media profile automatically confers on you 'a personal brand'. So you need to ensure that yours is well-conceived and clear. It helps to undertake a personal branding process that results in a focused *brand positioning statement* that articulates your unique value that you then leverage across your social media profiles.

**"Your personal brand is a promise to your clients...
a promise of quality, consistency, competency, and
reliability"**
Jason Hartman, American real estate and media
businessman

You can go through the process on your own, but there are more advantages to making this a team exercise where your colleagues and managers can provide their insights. Creating your personal brand should not be taken lightly and I strongly recommend taking time to research how best to do this, or to engage professional support.

It's important to note that your brand positioning statement is not just something that you want to tell others about yourself. Its purpose is to help build your credibility by telling others what you can do for them, and therefore it needs to be formulated from their perspective, not yours.

The first step is to reflect on your strengths, skills and talents. Ask those you work with to give you their opinions about the value you add and the qualities they find most worthwhile in you. This is important because we sometimes don't recognise a quality we have as significant, but it is to others.

The next step is to write your brand positioning statement. This is a short, focused 'sound bite' that clearly and concisely provides the answers to three questions:

1. Who are the people who benefit from your work?

2. What value can you deliver to them? (How do you help them?)

3. How do you do this differently from others with similar qualifications and experience?

In answering these questions, and in the writing of your personal brand positioning statement, it is important that you are authentic. Don't write what you think will impress people. Don't oversell yourself. Tell it like it is. Winning brands are always able to easily live up to the promise of their positioning statements. In addition, if you're honest in the way you present yourself through social media channels, you'll be confident when the time comes for face-to-face interactions.

From the brand positioning statement, you can also craft a personal brand tagline—and if you do, make sure it is smart, memorable, relative and true—for example mine is simply: 'business growth specialist'.

There are excellent publications devoted entirely to this topic, but below are a few tips to help you get started in building your personal brand:

Understand and be your authentic self

All too often I see salespeople not be themselves—they create a fake persona in the hope it will be more attractive to prospective clients or simply to 'stroke their own ego'. These people need to maintain a fake image and will eventually be caught out—in social media there is no place to hide. Your brand must be a reflection of who you are and with whom your prospects will actually connect.

People connect with other people and do business with those they know, like, trust and respect. If you don't appear to be a real person, or if it just looks like you're faking it, how likely do you think others are to trust you? Even if they do buy into your fake persona for a while, the slightest bit of inconsistency could prove problematic.

Building a personal brand is first and foremost developing an understanding of your true self, and then sharing that with the world.

Engage with your community

Seek out appropriate speaking engagements that will involve your target audience. Show that you are confident, approachable and know what you're talking about.

Write articles and participate in interviews. Write a blog and share it with your contacts. Write articles on LinkedIn and other social media platforms. LinkedIn offers the opportunity to write posts that are potentially seen by thousands of members of the social network. Write to position yourself as an expert in your field and don't be afraid to be controversial.

Engage in community group discussions on relevant social media platforms.

Build an online bank of references

Thanks to social media, people are going to be talking about you, your company and your services, whether you like it or not. Taking the lead with this in a positive manner will help you build relationships that will provide positive returns. As I keep emphasising, people buy from those they know, like, trust and respect. But while they might know and like you, how do they develop trust? Testimonials and references are a powerful means of overcoming any doubt in your prospects' mind. Ask your existing customers to provide quotes about their experiences with you personally and your company, and what you deliver. Use references that support your personal brand across your social media profiles. While these will not be the silver bullet to close sales, they will go a long way to helping build a trusting relationship.

Never Stop Learning

While it is likely you already have a good knowledge of your industry and your market, no matter how well you know your industry or area of expertise, things are changing at a faster rate than ever before and you have to stay up-to-date with the latest changes and trends.

It takes time to build your personal brand and if you fail to stay relevant, all of your effort will be wasted. If you don't want to be discredited, then you'll want to keep a steady supply of articles, trade journals, blogs, and books on hand.

It also pays to learn new things, develop new skills, and to expand your knowledge. If you're not growing, then you're stagnating, and that's the last thing you want to do as a successful salesperson.

It takes time and commitment to build your personal brand; it won't happen overnight. As you continue to develop your personal brand, stay consistent with your efforts, pay close attention to how your audience responds to your content, and hone your direction until your focus is on target.

Section 3
The Sales Cycle

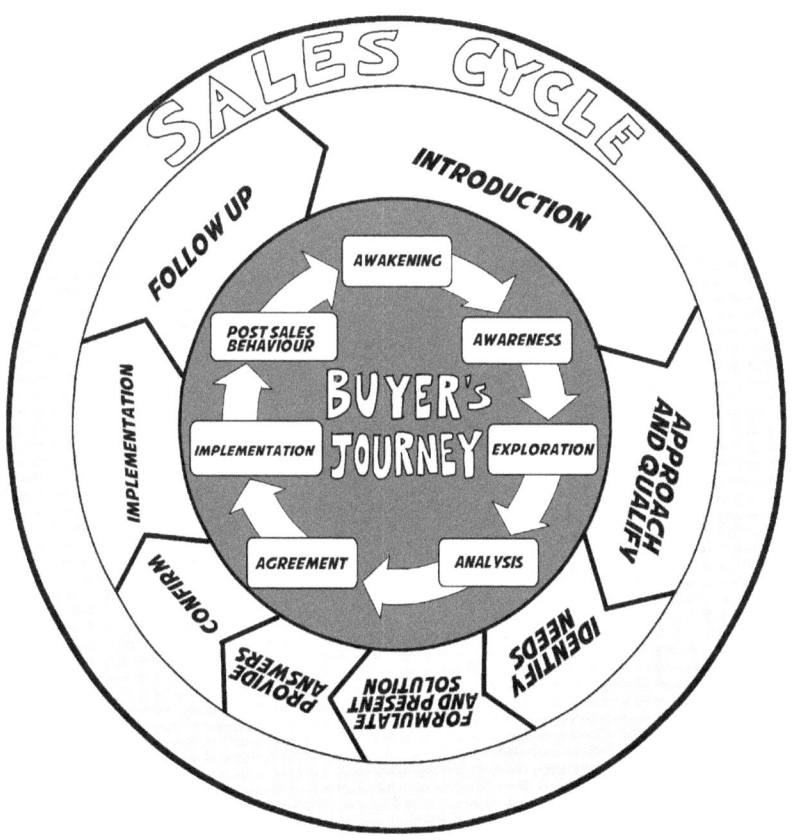

Now that we've looked at *what* makes a successful salesperson, let's look at *how* to be a successful salesperson.

The sales cycle is a process that you use to move step by step towards achieving sales—a mutually beneficial transaction. Every stage of the sales cycle offers you opportunities to build and sustain your relationship with prospects and clients. Understanding and following the sales cycle provides you with an organised and rational way to know where you stand with a prospect, and to assess what you need to do next to move forward with them towards your goal of delivering value.

It used to be that the process of making a sale was mostly dominated by the seller. That's all turned around nowadays, and it is the role of the salesperson being to integrate their sales cycle with the buyer's journey instead.

What is the buyer's journey?

There are a number of different definitions and models of the buyer's journey, but in general it describes the process a potential client moves through as they make decisions that will directly impact their final decision to engage with a salesperson by accepting your proposal. I find this simple definition most useful:

The Buyer's Journey

1. **Awakening** (and Awareness)
2. **Exploration**
3. **Analysis**
4. **Agreement**
5. **Implementation**
6. **Post-purchase behaviour**

It is becoming more and more common for a buyer to go through this entire journey on-line, especially in the B2C environment or when the transaction is seen as 'commodity-based'. However, even when that's not the case, it is estimated that B2B buyers can still be up to 70% through this journey online before they engage with a salesperson—that would mean that they have been awakened, they have explored and conducted a fair amount of analysis on their own.

In a B2B environment, it is not uncommon nowadays for the salesperson to 'physically' enter at stage three. However, recent research also shows that where an organisation IS engaged during the 'Awakening', they are 70% more likely to be successful. This means that the business' marketing efforts, as well as the personal 'branding' and networking of the salesperson must be closely aligned to the buyer's journey through stages one and two; the driving force behind the current call for sales and marketing to be far more integrated and collaborative than they have been before. Having a strong personal brand that is visible and active in relevant networks can increase a salesperson's opportunities to also be part of the buyer's journey through the awakening and exploration stages.

"Research shows that highly aligned B2B organizations achieve 19 percent faster revenue growth and 15 percent higher profitability."
Sirius Decisions, leading global B2B research and advisory firm

---

Let's understand these stages of the buyer's journey and how your company's communications need to strategically align to the different stages:

1. Awakening—your prospect has just become aware they have a need, but they may not yet be aware of the solution.

What needs to happen to be in alignment as the prospect awakens?

At this stage your business needs to be providing information that helps the prospective buyer understand the issue they face, gain a perspective on the impact and grow the awareness that they need to start exploring options. The content that has been delivered through both your company's marketing efforts and your own personal branding should help them begin thinking through insightful ways or options that might address their newly identified need—how they can solve their need. Your content should be based on commercial insight you have gained elsewhere—NOT simply on your product or service. While the information can be relatively generic, you need to be letting them know you can help them should they choose to move forward. What your business does to create awareness as the prospect awakens will differ depending on whether your context is B2C, B2B or a variation. It will also vary from industry to industry, market to market, but the goal remains the same—to get known and to influence thinking. While most of this effort will be the outputs of marketing, the salesperson does have a role to play through their personal brand. You can position yourself as a person with unique and valuable insight in your area by providing content such as videos, white papers, surveys or articles you have had published. It is also at this stage that more confident and prepared sales people should be able to challenge customers by presenting thoughts and ideas that may deliver opportunities or address problems not yet considered by the prospect or client.

2. Exploration—the buyer now acknowledges and accepts that they have a need that has to be, and can be satisfied; and now they are looking for options. From what you have presented during their awakening, they are aware that you are likely to be able to help them, but they know little about you and your offerings.

What needs to happen to be in alignment as the prospect explores?

This is the most critical part of the Buyer's Journey...and your sales process. It is is where you need be identifying the real needs of your prospective client. It is where you need to be continuing to deliver insight into what is happening in the market and how it will impact their business. But it goes beyond simply learning about their basic needs and 'what it might take to make the sale', real alignment will see the prospective client helping you understand what they need for them to do business with you and build a strong relationship. Having a sound exploration process will help you understand:

- What your prospective client is trying to achieve and what will drive them to change, to consider something new.

- What impact the issues have/may have on their business or individually.

- Their competitive environment

- Who your competition is, what other alternatives are possibly being considered and why.

- Their decision making process (DMP—how will they evaluate your proposal and those of other suppliers) and decision making unit (DMU—those going to be responsible for the decision to recommend/purchase)

- Importantly, the impact of maintaining the status quo— risk and lost opportunity.

- How the purchase will be justified and funded.

You need to continue to provide quality, more in-depth information about your company, product or services, the value you can deliver (as it will be defined by the client) and how it can specifically solve the issues being faced by the buyer, or deliver greater benefits. Marketing content once again plays a pivotal role in this stage, but so does the salesperson's personal brand. Through your professional profiles you present references and offer information that the buyer may not think they need, but will help position you as someone who can deliver value as defined by the prospect…

3. Analysis—the buyer has moved beyond the exploration stage and has become aware that you can deliver a suitable solution. At this stage, they are likely to want to compare you with other suppliers who are also under consideration.

What needs to happen to be in alignment as the prospect analyses?

This is typically the stage when the B2B salesperson begins physically interacting with the prospect. It is the start of your effort to ensure that the prospect can like, trust and respect you, and your company. Your personal brand may be what has helped you to get the prospect to engage with you. However, if they haven't come across you on-line by this stage, you can expect that they will now be visiting your profiles and assessing your credentials and information-sharing as part of their analysis. Your communication now needs to include content that shows not just the features, but most importantly, the benefits of your solution. You need to be able to simply and clearly articulate the *value* you can offer them—and from their perspective—not yours. If you know your market and your competition, you should be able to highlight your strengths and show the prospect how they will get the best through a relationship with you. It is a good time to provide case studies that show you can 'walk the talk'.

4. Agreement—yes, it's time. The buyer is ready to commit, so make it easy for them to choose you. They have acknowledged you can deliver the right solution, can do it at least as well as the others on the short list and provide greater value, so make this last step as simple as possible and let them feel good about their choice.

What needs to happen to be in alignment when the prospect agrees?

Make it easy. Whether that is to purchase online or engage with you personally, the easier it is for them to do so, the higher your chance of success. Provide relevant and credible testimonials if necessary and appropriate; show that your business is strong and will be there to support them if needed by sharing some of your vision for the business. Provide relevant but non-invasive follow-up communications that will be appreciated by the buyer and enhance your chance of future business.

5. Implementation (exchange of value)—While your sales cycle needs to appropriately intersect with the buyer's journey at each stage, it is arguably most important for this to happen here in order to ensure that you see that what you have sold to them delivers the value they expected, and you presented.

While implementation is not generally the domain of the salesperson; to walk away and abdicate responsibility for delivery of the value you have sold is both irresponsible and threatening to future business. Recent research suggests this is a problem among salespeople, with only around 25% of buyers saying their salesperson kept in touch during the exchange of value. Of more concern, only 30% of buyers said they received what they believed they had been sold and 10% claimed they never received what was promised.

What needs to happen to be in alignment when the buyer is exchanging value?

It is up to you to build internal networks with the people in your organisation who are responsible for implementation. You need to keep them abreast of the pending sale, make sure they are fully briefed on the expectations you have set and that they deliver what you have promised. Also, keeping in touch with the buyer during this stage will help ensure a high level of customer satisfaction.

6. Post-purchase behaviour—The buyer has just completed one of the many journeys to purchase that they will take. How you managed this trip, how well you integrated the sales cycle with their buyer's journey and how you follow-up will determine whether they will be with you on the next venture once they return again to stage one. It also impacts on whether they would recommend you to others who are about to start on a similar path.

While the process defined here will apply in general to any B2B sale, managing complex sales will require more detailed analysis of each and every step and an approach that has a very clear and well-defined strategy.

You must also note that the alignment of the buyer's journey and the sales cycle is 'slippery'. Rarely will the two align identically from one opportunity to another. The successful sales professional will become adept at understanding how to bring the two together to ensure value is delivered at every stage.

With this understanding of the road a buyer typically travels, we can move on to looking at the sales cycle that you follow in detail.

What is important to accept is that the buyer's journey is just that. It is THEIR journey, not yours. You need to fit in.

Lead Generation

There is a quote in business that has been attributed to many people over the years… *"Nothing happens until someone sells something"*

But from a sales perspective, the reality is…

Nothing happens until you generate a lead!

This first stage of our sales cycle is a 'research and development' phase where we explore, investigate and discover where our ideal client can be found and how best to make contact with them in ways that make them want to enter into a relationship with us.

In many businesses, the responsibility of lead generation is shared with marketing. In recent times, the lines between sales and marketing have become blurred with the result that companies with collaborative marketing and sales environments are proving to be more successful. The more informed and co-ordinated our lead generation strategies are, the better our chances of finding leads that actually turn into prospects.

Effective lead generation relies on a bundle of integrated methods to reach the target market. How you generate leads can vary from person to person, business to business, industry to industry and market to market. For these strategies to be effective, you need to first clearly define and understand who you want to sell to. Don't think about who might buy from you; instead, know exactly who you can deliver value to through the offering of your expertise, and your product or service.

Methods of Lead Generation

This overview of lead generation techniques presents some of the typical methods used. However, lead generation activities are not at all limited to standard practices. While innovations are constantly being presented by technological changes, the creativity of individual marketing and salespeople also plays a major role in this fundamental phase of the sales cycle. It is up to you to understand and utilise a variety of tried and tested strategies that suit your industry, as well as to introduce methods that work for you as an individual.

- **Social Media**

Social media is already being well-used to generate leads, and this is only going to increase in time. As an emerging force, there is an ever-increasing number of tools that can be used to find out who is engaging in particular topics across a multitude of industries on different social media sites. The rate of development of these platforms and tools makes recommendations in print redundant. Examples of this, at this time, include Twitter's 'website cards' and Slideshare's 'Pro Plan' which help you to build relevant lead lists.

You need to explore the options, get recommendations from current users and choose the tools that help you show up and engage in the preferred media of your ideal client. LinkedIn has made a major impact on lead generation, and writing and publishing content on LinkedIn helps to develop and showcase your personal brand— the unique promise of value you present to your target customers. Depending on where you can find your ideal client, you may also consider developing a Facebook profile that is about you the professional, opting in to Twitter and Google+ lead generation tools, optimising the content marketing on your company's website and redesigning the user experience on your company's website to simplify and emphasise a simple and vital call to action in order to generate more leads (an area where sales and marketing need to collaborate). Right now, social media is a frontier world in lead generation—it already delivers results and there is no doubt that its use in will increase, and increase rapidly.

- **Cold and Warm Calling**

Personally, I hate 'traditional' cold calling as it's impossible to hold your status as a business equal during this type of interaction. However, I recognise in certain businesses and in particular industries; targeted, appropriate and skilful cold calling and telemarketing are valid and practical lead generation techniques.

If cold calling can get you the results that you need, bear the following in mind:

- **You still need to be targeted**—you can't just call 'anyone', you have to call the people who you can add value to for this process to be efficient and effective
- **Don't start low**—if it is a B2B situation, get to the decision-maker or as near as possible on your first call. Use this contact to be introduced to others key individuals in the organisation.

- **Keep the goal in mind**—you are at the start of the sales cycle, the opposite end from securing a sale. The initial (cold or otherwise) call is an introduction, not a 'closing'

- **Be relevant**—quickly demonstrate that you understand this person's present challenges and have a potential solution, or that you understand their business and have an offer that will deliver value

- **Don't damage your brand**—cold calling has the risk of annoying people and they can associate annoyance with your brand.

"If opportunity doesn't knock, build a door"
Milton Berle (1908—2002), American comedian and actor

- **Warming it up**

Even when cold calling is applicable, I recommend warming up first. By doing more in-depth research on potential opportunities and being far more targeted by thoroughly considering which individual should be approached by geography, industry, market or role, you are empowered to engage at a more credible level. Warming up the cold call is vital when the sale is more complicated and valuable. Social media offers lots of new opportunities to turn a cold call warm. Connecting via a professional platform first enables you to deliver articles of interest and specific direct marketing so that your cold call is not so cold. Your referral program and other networks can also help you to warm up a cold call for greater effect. While it takes more time and effort, sending the lead something before you call such as an event invitation, 'business-worthy' information, a special offer, an introductory email message or some promotional gift can help to take the harsh edge off a plain cold call, and it gives you something to follow up on as an opening statement. Once you are on the call it is important to allow the conversation to flow naturally and to watch for 'signposts' that enable to you discover if there is common ground between you and the lead. These signposts should take the form of exploratory questions rather than be ways for you to move the lead towards the 'next step' of the sales process. Pushing your agenda on a cold call will almost always result in them hurrying you off the line.

- **Trigger Event Prospecting**

Like so many things in life, success in sales can be all about timing. Contacting a prospect just after they have purchased from a competitor will deliver little chance of success. Likewise, contacting them when they have recently outsourced services that you compliment will unlikely generate any interest.

Traditional prospecting often meant our timing was just not right and all too often was the result of 'luckily' being in the right place at the right time. Fortunately, with the help of social media salespeople can not just talk to their prospects, but listen as well. 'Triggers' are events that set off, or are likely to set off activity within your prospect or client. These may be changes in management, for example, the introduction of a new CEO with a reputation for cost-cutting or maybe one with whom you have had previous successful relationships. Perhaps they have announced a recent acquisition, office opening or launched a new product or service. Have there been industry events that might impact the way they should be doing business? Has there been recent negative or positive market reaction to something within the prospect's business or industry?

Trigger events typically come in three different forms.

1. **Problem Indicators:** Information suggesting your prospect/client (or the industry generally) may be struggling with issues that *you and/or your offering can resolve*

2. **Opportunity Indicators:** Information highlighting goals & objectives your prospect/client is trying to achieve *that you can help them achieve*

3. **Change/Transition**: Information suggesting the company/ industry is experiencing some sort of change or transition that you and your offering can assist with. This type of trigger event represents change in the company such as hiring a new CEO or executive or a recent merger and acquisition.

'Listening' on social media can be time-consuming and counter-productive if it takes you away from actually 'selling'. Fortunately with social media salespeople can listen 'automatically' to their target markets. While the apps that allow 'social-listening' will be always changing, here are a few that help with the core elements of listening:

- **Social Listening**—Tools like Hootsuite, TweetDeck and Social Mention can give you a heads up when prospects are discussing your company on various social media sites like LinkedIn or Twitter.

- **News Alerts**—Google Alerts, Mentioned and Awario will all send you notifications about recent news focused on a company or individual you're keeping an eye on.

- **Email Tracking**—Yesware, Vocus and other tools can let you know when a prospect has opened your email.

- **LinkedIn Navigator**—will let you know when there is any company or individual activity on people you have nominated as a 'lead'.

When you follow trigger events you need to do so in a timely manner—act fast. By using 'triggers', successful salespeople can engage with prospects at the right time—the time they are most likely to have an interest in engaging with you. Triggers allow you the opportunity to send relevant information to your prospect/client and to engage with them on a level that does not involve directly trying to sell something. Effectively using trigger events relieves pressure on the salesperson because they shouldn't feel like they have to "sell" something but instead can focus the conversation on the trigger event and the prospect/client and helping the customer with his/her thought process.

- **Proactive Referral Program**

Successful salespeople don't hope for referrals, they have a program that is planned and managed on an ongoing basis, because this is a highly effective way of reaching your ideal client.

The people in your networks, who are willing to share their contacts with you, refer and recommend you, and empower you to use their name to open doors, are VIPs in your working life. They can help you to quickly turn suspects into hot prospects. They can lead you into new, plentiful territories. They are influencers on your side, on your path to success. Your relationships with them are as important as your connections to current clients.

There are two important aspects of your referral program:

- Gathering and collating the contacts who may or have referred you
- Devising and implementing a contact plan where you regularly touch-base in the most appropriate ways with those who may or have referred you

Relevant referrals can come from any quarter—past clients and current clients; friends and family; your gym buddy, your banjo teacher or your blog follower; the principal at your kid's school or your sky-diving instructor... You cannot sit back and hope that 'something might happen'. It is up to you to take an interest in who the people you know, know. It is up to you to let them know what you do and to nurture the authentic relationships that makes them want to refer you. Obviously, asking your current clients for referrals to businesses that may have similar needs for your service or products seems as if it is the most targeted approach, but don't disregard more surprising connections. Put these into your referral program, for exploration, discovery and introduction.

Another important way to positively develop your referral program is to pay attention to your personal brand. Brands help referrals and referrals help brand development. By actively promoting both your personal and company brands you can increase your visibility and credibility, creating favourable conditions to attract targeted referrals.

There are 4 important points to remember in referring business:

1. Be prepared to give before you get
2. Don't expect it to happen overnight, it's an investment
3. Make sure your referrals are relevant, to all parties
4. Follow up and acknowledge the referrals you receive

I enjoy working with smaller businesses wanting to become bigger businesses—my focus always being on business development. Both personally and on-line I have developed close relationships with other service providers who target the same businesses—accountants, financial planners and insurance brokers. Through these relationships I have gained many valuable introductions that have led to significant business, especially as the business grows. But most importantly, I have reciprocated with appropriate introductions of my own.

- **Direct Marketing**

This is a long-established lead generation technique, traditionally associated with 'snail' mail or some form of physical delivery. It was usually the responsibility of marketing rather than sales. However, with the trend nowadays that demands businesses be more targeted and relevant, it helps for sales and marketing to collaborate to ensure that direct marketing efforts reach the people who are actually interested in our product or service because it will genuinely add value to them. Sales need to be communicating with marketing the 'word on the street', what it is that the market is looking for and what 'value' they want. All too often marketing efforts are wasted on promoting features and benefits when what the market is looking for is the value that can be generated. It's the responsibility of sales to know what this is and communicate it to the rest of the company.

Direct marketing is also now done electronically (email) rather than 'pen and paper' and developing strong email lists will help you reach more of your ideal clients. In the past direct marketing was very much a shotgun approach, which is still widely used in a B2C environment. However, we are now living in an age of content overload and particularly in the B2B context you need take up the rifle. You don't have to be a sniper, but the 'direct marketing' approach needs to be far more direct in today's market, and it needs to be relevant.

- **Networking**

Your networking activities obviously overlap with just about all the lead generation techniques we've discussed so far. Today, networking happens both off and on-line. It is all about establishing your credible presence in your spheres of business influence. This lead generation method is all about you and your reputation as an individual. Social media platforms present your best opportunities to network online. Developing your strong personal brand online is essential. You have vast scope to present your credentials as an expert, trusted and valued advisor. Being active and engaging, relevant and sharing can all help you to stand out in the busy online environment and to develop a network that supports you in generating leads. But don't forget the off-line environment.

And most importantly, do NOT sell when networking, either on or off-line. Networking should be about building your profile and personal brand; establishing trust.

"The currency of real networking is not greed but generosity"
Keith Ferrazzi, American author and founder/CEO of
research institute and consulting firm, Ferrazzi Greenlight

- **Events**

One of the consequences of our increasing on-line activity is that it sheds the spotlight on events that enable real, personal connections. Industry meetings and conferences, trade shows and expos have actually become more prized as more people feel the value of face-to-face interaction and engagement beyond the connectivity of a device.

If you are ready for it, seek out opportunities to speak and present. You can also optimise the opportunities offered by relevant events by researching delegates and exhibitors beforehand so that you can strategically network with those most in your target market or those most likely to further your lead generation efforts.

Attending relevant events also helps you to keep up to date with what is happening in your industry, which enables you to be more effective in generating leads. It will also present networking opportunities—these lead generation ideas are not necessarily independent of each other.

- **Reactivating old prospects**

Think about the principle of 'leaving no one behind'. Maintaining contact with past clients and prospects can help you identify future opportunities and assist with referrals. I currently use a program, 'Contactually', where I place contacts in 'buckets' according to their status such as client, past client, prospect, referral partner etc. Then I set time-frames for contact. This gives me daily reminders to make contact, and it is essentially a more sophisticated and efficient system of doing just what I used to do with a business card file.

People were similarly ranked, and then I used a spreadsheet to record points of contact. Whatever you do needs to work for you, and it doesn't necessarily need to be sophisticated.

Stage Two
Approach and Qualify

Suspects or prospects?

While it can be said that 'nothing happens until you have a lead'; a lead is only of value if it is qualified, then managed into and through your sales process.

Throughout my career, as a salesperson, a sales manager and consultant on sales development, this is where I have seen most businesses getting the sales process wrong. All too often, businesses look to generate as many leads as possible, and then they waste time on those that are unlikely to deliver a positive return on further investment.

"A daring beginning is halfway to winning."
Heinrich Heine (1797—1856); German poet

Leads are the raw material of sales

If we consider sales as a process, like any other process there are inputs and outputs. Leads are the raw material of the sales process and as in manufacturing, if the raw materials are wrong or of poor quality, a poor finished product will result. This raw material, the lead, needs to be turned into a finished product, a sale.

Qualifying your opportunities is like putting your raw material through quality control. It helps sort the wheat from the chaff and focus on the business you can win. It prevents you from wasting your time chasing business you can't, or are very unlikely to win. In the present moment, you want to know the difference between 'suspects' and 'prospects' so that you can commit your energy to the latter.

Prospects are people who have been screened for their level of interest in what you offer and have passed your qualification criteria. They are people to whom you or your support team, have decided you have a good chance of delivering value. Experienced salespeople have techniques for how to check out enquiries to determine whether the suspect/prospect is serious or 'just shopping' which usually takes the form of a series of careful questions. There is no template for these questions as they will differ from business to business, and market to market.

However, the answers to your questions should give you an idea of the prospect's 'sales readiness' and enable you to determine how much effort you are going to have to put into this lead, as well as how you need to adapt your approach to suit them as buyer. It's a time of discovery that calls for heightened awareness. You need to observe and listen accurately and fully. For instance, if you misread a lead as really hot when they are actually just starting to get interested, you might push your case a little more aggressively than they feel comfortable with. Similarly, if you misread a hot client as warm or cold, you could be perceived as offhand with the result that they lose their interest in you.

Here are some overarching tips for qualifying prospects:

- Know your ideal client—this is not a person who may buy from you, but a person or business to whom you can deliver value

- Stay attuned to the messages from leads that might indicate they could become a prospect

- Observe and listen; analyse and understand the information you have gathered

- Shift your mindset from trying to 'close a sale' to creating more openings for valuable information to flow and deeper connections to be made

- Keep your focus on the needs of your lead—it's not about whether they might buy and help you reach your target; it's about whether you can deliver a quality solution that adds value to them

How many prospects convert to sales?

To some extent, this transactional sales formula is always applicable; however, it will be less applicable the more complex and higher value the sales opportunity. Salespeople need to know their own ratios, and their business should be tracking the best/worst/average so that individuals can benchmark themselves. Knowing these numbers allows salespeople to put their effort where it is needed. Working to improve qualification and conversion means that fewer suspects are required to make your target. For example:

100%	suspects, convert to
50%	prospects, who provide the
25%	best few, who deliver YOUR SALES

You can improve this ratio, and your efficiency through:

- Better qualification
- Better prospect management
- Better confirmation of the sale (ie closing)

Building Rapport

To accurately qualify a lead, you need to get to know those involved in the decision-making process (DMP). It is not at all unusual for a potential client to be somewhat wary of you at your first face-to-face meeting. You have to quickly and easily provide the assurance that their reservations are unnecessary. Salespeople who steamroll into their 'pitch' at the first opportunity they have to speak are mostly likely to just waste their and the buyer's time on a meeting that won't go anywhere. Your aim needs to be to make a direct, honest connection and build rapport. Sharing a quick, appropriate personal note or professional insight; asking non-intrusive questions or inviting comment and opinion can open up a conversation that leads to discovering something about the buyer's interests and points of view, as well as help you to identify their style or find something you have in common. Developing rapport-building skills and experience is essential for salespeople. It is something that you should be actively doing with suspects, prospects and even, well-established clients at just about every contact point. It is a way of connecting to a person that enables you to be constantly learning something new about them, and the better you know a person, the easier it is to deliver value to them. Taking a genuine interest in the person behind the labels 'suspect'/'prospect'/'client' underpins building real rapport with them.

Who's Doing the Buying?

One of the first things that you want to qualify about your lead is whether you are talking to the person with the power to make a buying decision. In more complex sales, there will usually be a number of individuals in the decision-making unit (DMU), which is often cross-departmental—some of these influencers may be formal, others informal; some you may know, others you don't; some may be on your side, others won't. But you can be sure, the more complex and higher value the sale, the more people who will be involved.

Some of the formal roles in the buying process might include:

- User
- Evaluator
- Decision-maker
- Approver

You want to use the early points of contact with your lead to discover as much as possible as to who is involved, and how their buying process works. The aim of this information gathering is so that you:

- know the formal decision criteria
- understand the informal decision criteria
- understand your current relationship
- gain inside support
- achieve political alignment

In order to qualify your lead as accurately as possible, you also want to reflect on and assess your status with other key players in their organisation. This evaluation is an ongoing process as you move through the sales cycle and deepen your relationship with the lead.

- **Coach**—this is someone who is personally invested in your success and works actively and openly to champion you getting the sale. They are likely to share insider information with you, help you to develop and test your sales plan, and they may take on the accountability for implementing your solution.

- **Fan**—this is a person who prefers your solution and wants you to succeed, but they keep that support private. They are likely to provide you with helpful information if you ask for it.

- **Ambivalent**—this key player agrees that a solution needs to be found and that yours may be a suitable fit, but they express no preferences. They may be ambivalent about the options on offer or are choosing to present a neutral façade.

- **Non-supporter**—this is someone who doesn't think you should get the sale or prefers a competitive offer.

- **Nemesis**—this person may well take actions to see you lose the sale as they believe your solution may be detrimental to the organisation or themselves. They may be a coach or fan of your competition.

Targeting the decision-makers

You may have put a lot of effort into securing a face-to-face meeting with a lead, only to quickly discover they don't play a part in the decision-making process. They may still be able to help you find out who is, and how the organisation's buying process works, as well as give you introductions and referrals within the organisation. However, it helps to be targeting the influencers and decision-makers from the start.

You can identify decision makers through:

- satisfied customers—who made the decisions and what process was followed in your successful sales?

- prospects who don't buy—why did they not buy? Did you not understand their value requirement, were your engaging the wrong people?

- centres of influence

- business acquaintances, friends—leverage your contacts who might be able to introduce you to the 'right' people in an organisation

- going to the top—with a strong value proposition, a well developed personal brand and knowledge of the business and market, pitching to the senior management in an organisation can then allow you to be introduced 'down the line' to those who will drive the project

While it may seem that this information is very hard to come by, there are a number of strategies you can use:

- embrace 'social selling' and develop a strong, effective online profile by positioning yourself as an expert in your field to build your credibility

- use social media platforms such as LinkedIn to help identify influencers and decision-makers. Be aware of who you may know who could identify and connect you to decision-makers

- nurture relationships with, and gather information from gatekeepers

- ask for guidance from friends and business associates who may have knowledge of your lead's organization

- get as high up the organisational structure as you can and ask to be referred down to those who will influence the buying decision—to do this you need to provide a good reason for the upper managers to engage with you

- learn from past successes and failures—who made the decisions, and why?

- conduct win/loss reviews with the customer and your team—many businesses are happy to do this as it helps them get better service and ensures a more competitive supply chain
- keep ongoing records such as purchase history, delivery and payment preferences

Qualifying Potential Prospects

Not all prospects are ready to buy. Historical statistics show that 30% of sales engagements end in 'no decision'. This figure has no doubt decreased as potential buyers do more online research and not engage with the salesperson as early, but nonetheless, not all prospects will be real prospects.

So, let's get rid of those who are wasting your time, so that you can concentrate on getting more than your fair share of the real opportunities. Qualifying is the process of separating out the tyre-kickers. It bridges the gap between the quantity of leads and their quality.

Qualifying the simple sale

A 'simple' sale is the one-off sale of a product or service to an individual person or business. Using a scripted set of qualifying questions, the suspect's responses should enable you to determine within the first meeting whether or not the person you're talking with is really a promising prospect. These questions are obviously going to differ from industry to industry. While you want to ask some generic open-ended questions; you also want to use targeted questions that draw on your knowledge of your particular business or market. For example: "I have clients in this industry who are experiencing issues with…How is this impacting on your business right now?"

Qualifying more complex sales

The complex sale is usually a B2B transaction that involves a more protracted buying decision process involving a number of people in such formal roles as the user, the evaluator, the decision-maker and the approver. Often, there are also informal influencers in the mix. As we've discussed before, you need to identify the players and have a good idea where you stand with them. You also need to assess their readiness to purchase so that you know how quickly and thoroughly you need to start acting. Your questions in this scenario will include those to find out whether they are currently evaluating a product or service such as yours and why they are in the market for it, as well as whether budget has been committed and whether they intend purchasing soon or are they still a long way out.

Methods of Qualifying Prospects

Here are three methods that that you can use to qualify prospects:

1. The 'Temperature' Rating Method

This is the simplest method and is included for completeness. It is not a method that will stand up to strong interrogation, nonetheless, it has proven effective to experienced salespeople since salespeople started to approach their job in a professional manner. Once you have an idea of their buying readiness you can tag your leads as 'hot', 'warm', 'cold':

- **'Hot'** are those who are definitely looking to buy
- **'Warm'** are those who might buy
- **'Cold'** are probably not interested in buying at this time

Naturally you concentrate your efforts on the 'Hot' prospects. Give them priority and convert them to sales as quickly as possible. Never leave a 'Hot' prospect to give attention to a 'Cold' one. Only after all the 'Hot' contacts have been processed should you turn your attention to 'Warm' ones. 'Cold' are hardly ever worth pursuing unless no other contacts can be obtained—and if the only contacts you have aren't interested in buying from you, you're in need of a new system of lead generation!

2. BANTA Lead Scoring

The BANT method has been used for many years and provides a greater level of accuracy, but also requires more effort—effort that will be well-rewarded. It requires you to be more involved with the opportunity so that you get to know them, ask more detailed questions and do greater research.

- **Budget**

  Is it available and approved?

- **Authority**

  Is your lead a decision-maker, influencer, user, approver?

- **Need**

  Do they have a confirmed need that you can solve? Are you able to offer value they may or may not see? Can you give them a reason to want to change?

- **Timing**

  Do they have a need that must be satisfied in a specific time? Can you create a compelling reason to purchase in a specific time? For example, will your solution help them to implement improvements before peak season?

- **Attractiveness (Value)**

  I have added 'A' to the traditional acronym to depict the attractiveness or value of your offer.

  How attractive/valuable is your offer to them? To determine this, answer questions such as these: Is the prospect's application or project clearly defined? Can we address this? Do we solve a problem or deliver 'gain'? Do we add any unique value? What is the ROI that will be delivered? What is the cost of the value you will deliver—monetary, risk and the cost of implementation

Rate each question according to the following scale:

Very weak	———————	0
Weak	———————	1
OK	———————	2
Good	———————	3
Strong	———————	4
Very strong	———————	5

Low scores indicate either an opportunity not worth pursuing or, possibly, the need for you to do greater research. The low score may be a result of you not knowing the answer.

Once you are comfortable you have researched the opportunity fully and you have provided final and accurate response, very strong and strong equate to 'hot' prospects that you attend to immediately; good and OK equate to 'warm' prospects that you deal with next; and, weak and very weak are the 'cold' prospects who you should leave alone. It must be noted that qualifying is not a 'once-off' exercise. You need to be asking these questions throughout your sales cycle.

3.   Wayne's Litmus Test

Will your lead pass my *Litmus Test*?

Not all leads are opportunities and not all opportunities can be won. The *Litmus Test* is a little more detailed than BANTA and again helps you filter out the good leads from the bad—those to drop, those to chase and those you might want to 'park for later'.

1. **Has the prospect got a need?** Is there a need for the products and services you are selling? Does the prospect have a problem you can solve? Does your product/service/solution help them generate more business? Do you understand their need? If in doubt, check it out. If the prospect is serious, they will share information with you that will help you deliver the best solution. If they don't, that's the first 'red flag'. Remember, in today's market there is little to differentiate one product or service from another, however you and your business are unique; your products have different benefits, your business has a different competitive advantage. You have your own unique strengths, and way of packaging a solution. Make sure they understand your solution and that it is what they want and need. Sometimes what the customer wants is actually not what they need. One of the ways salespeople add value is by packaging what the client needs with what they want—so you are selling them what they want and giving them what they need. It's quite easy to assign a score to this by understanding how much pain they are in and what are the consequences of not resolving the issue or erasing the pain. Or conversely, the increased sales or profit your solution might create for the prospect.

    Selling your value may mean you need to create a need for your prospect by challenging the way they currently do business. And this may mean engaging with non-traditional contacts within an organisation.

    There was a time in my sales career I was involved in the launch of the first 'value-add' telecommunications services to a previously monopolised market. The features offered were not going to be of interest to the traditional buyers, the communications managers, but would provide significant marketing advantage and increased customer satisfaction. One of our target customers was a cruise line and our focus needed to be on the Yield Manager, Sales and Marketing Managers as well as the COO. Once these individuals were convinced of the value we could add to their business, the differentiation they would gain in the market and improvements in service delivery they could achieve, they put together a team to evaluate the proposal and we were effectively writing our own RFQ.

2. **Is there a compelling reason for change?** For people to make a decision they normally need two things—a compelling reason to change and a specific event by which they must make a decision. Without both these in place decisions can drift on forever.

   What is driving the customer to make a decision or a change in the current situation? What is the event that will force a decision by a particular time? It could be budget approval date, a board meeting, a company press briefing or a stock market briefing. What is the payback if they make a change? What are the consequences if they do not act? If there is no compelling event, the urgency to make a decision can delay the sales process and waste your time. Compelling events can be based on issues faced by the prospect, or created.

   After I helped launch a new telecommunications company, the biggest benefit we delivered was reduced costs and we could offer new clients savings. For the Communications Manager, this did not create a compelling event. If he did not make a decision to change and he continued to do the same as always, the company missed out on the savings, but his budget was still in order and he avoided risk. We needed to change tack and instead sell the savings that could be achieved to the CFO and CEO. When we added that the offer had a sunset clause, suddenly there was a compelling event.

3. **When do they need it?** What specific date is associated with the compelling event? What is their timing? When does the problem have to be solved? When does the target need to be met? If it isn't urgent then are they really looking for a solution now? If there is no urgency, treat the opportunity as 'suspect', keep in touch for when they may be ready, but don't waste time that could be better spent.

4. **Do you know the prospect's decision-making process?** If you don't know who and how the decisions are made within the prospect's business, and if you are not dealing with the right people, then this will score low. If you cannot get to the right people, it's a strong indication you will struggle to close the deal—it's a low score.

5. **Is there future opportunity with this prospect?** Is there a strategic reason or long-term gain for winning this business? If you win this business what other opportunities might you be able to uncover? Does this company have affiliates or contacts that may be useful in the future? Is it part of a larger organisation that, if you do well here, might lead to greater opportunities? You don't want to spend a lot of time and expense on a small deal at low margin if you can't see any way to sell something else in the future.

6. **Can they afford you?** The prospect may have a need, may be the right person, and may even be willing, but without the money, your sale won't happen. Determine that the prospect has the necessary budget for your service (or can you present a way for them to finance the proposal). They may not tell you their budget but you can usually get an indication and also get confirmation that a clear budget has been approved. And remember, by positioning your solution to solve a problem or create an opportunity, the question can be turned into "Can they afford NOT to work with you?"

7. **Can you support them?** Depending on the type of product or service you are selling, this can be a non-issue or critical. You need to be able to service the sale. Is this done remotely (internet or phone) or do you need to do it personally? And it's not just location. Do you speak their language, both literally and figuratively? If your product or service is a critical part of the client's supply chain, support may be a very significant part of their decision. How you provide

follow-up service can make or break your business, especially in today's world of social media. Be realistic.

8. **Have they got the skills to use it?** This is often overlooked, but is very important. Have they got the right skills and sponsorship to implement your solution? You want them to implement your solution, have positive outcomes and be a great reference.

Use the following rating scale to assign a value to each of the eight questions:

1. *Very Weak*
2. *Weak*
3. *OK*
4. *Good*
5. *Strong*
6. *Very Strong*

How did you score?

You will have a result from 0 to 48

Total Score: _____

Score 0 to 16—Drop it

If you scored less than 16 forget it. It's hard to say 'NO' but don't waste your time. Spend the time on the opportunities you can win and not those you can't. A prospect list is just a sales funnel and not everything can go through. So don't try to force poor leads into opportunities—let go early! You must give your time to the few that will return rewards, not the many that will waste your time.

Score 17 to 32—Gather more information

You need to ask a few more probing questions before you decide.

Score 33 plus—Chase

If you scored more than 33 the opportunity is well qualified and deserves your time. But even if you scored above 33 and had a low score on several questions, you need to discover more information in those areas.

With your opportunity qualified 'in' or 'out', put together a sales plan to target the business. If it is real, be committed to the opportunity and gain internal support to engage the necessary resources to win the deal. Make sure you understand what the prospect sees as value and work to deliver this. By working on less opportunities and adding more value, you will win more business.

Knowing when to walk away

Wasting time with a 'prospect' who isn't going to buy from you means less time working on real opportunities.

"You've got to know when to hold 'em, know when to fold 'em".
Johnny Cash (1932—2003), American singer-songwriter

I use 4 simple questions to decide where to put my valuable time:

1. Is there a REAL problem or opportunity? Can you show the prospect a reason to engage? Can you show them that you can deliver value to their business? Does the prospect have a problem that needs to be solved or a desire to grow? Do you understand these? Do they have the budget? Do they have a compelling reason to make a decision?

2. Can you compete? Can you solve their problem or satisfy their desire/need? Do you have an existing relationship (compared to you competitors)?

3. Can you win? Are you seen as a serious contender? Do you have inside support and market credibility? Do you understand the decision-making process? Does the prospect trust you?

4. Is it worth winning? If you win, is the deal going to be profitable? Is there longer-term strategic value in winning the deal?

Answering "no" to any of these questions should set off an alarm. Dig deeper to decide whether this is an opportunity worth your valuable time, effort and resources. And, don't think this only applies to B2B sales, quick qualifying in B2C sales can also mean more revenue and better profits.

Today, in B2B sales you can't afford to waste time with opportunities that do not have a great potential to deliver results. Your busy prospects and clients do not want the deal with suppliers who waste their time.

You need to be working to minimise waste and adding value. This is the essence of 'lean selling', and it ultimately creates more capacity for you to focus on real opportunities. And the greatest time-waster is paying attention to opportunities that have little or no real potential. **This is the compelling reason to qualify fast… and, qualify early…**

Sometimes, you might resist walking away from a lead, especially one that you have chased hard. You need to remember that a lead will ultimately respect you more for not wasting their time. There may well come a future time when that same person will be a 'hot' prospect for the value you have to offer. You want to walk away in the present on respectful, rational and positive terms, so that you are in good standing when an opportunity might arise for a return.

> **"Your competition is EVERYTHING else your prospect
> could conceivably spend money on"**
> Don Cooper, American sales trainer

Managing your sales 'lifeline'

Ongoing management of enquiries and leads can sometimes be daunting, but some of the following tips can help you stay on top of the information and be well-organised:

- Don't let enquiries and leads pile up. Tackle them and record them as soon as possible while the information is fresh in your mind. This is a task that can be outsourced, if necessary.

- Qualify the enquiries and leads as to your ability to deliver value and their propensity to purchase. Which ones are hot, warm or cold? Prioritise your hot leads and handle them immediately.

- Once you follow-up with an enquiry or lead, upgrade them to a contact—someone who gets regular mailings and special offers.

- Update your records regularly as you develop a history with a customer—know their purchase history and personal tastes so that you can provide the best customer service.

Sales Lead Follow Up

Slow, or no response to leads means lost opportunities. This is yet another area where sales and marketing need to be collaborating, with sales providing useful feedback to marketing so the support materials they provide are adequate and appropriate.

You can increase your effectiveness by being well-prepared:

- have different materials to send in response to different types of enquiries. Not simply brochures but information that will help educate the prospect and demonstrate you understand their business, such as white papers and case studies.

- have electronic versions to email and on your website

- keep adequate supplies of printed materials ready for those who prefer them

- have the people, systems and processes in place to get the requested information out the door quickly

- make it easy for prospects to get in touch with you— addresses and email on all marketing materials and a high profile personal brand online

As part of your lead planning and generation process you need to think a bit down the track too—how are you going to handle the enquiries that come in? For a start, you ought to be able to move fast. Leads are like fresh produce: they spoil quickly. Though figures vary from study to study the overall finding for medium to large businesses is always the same—in these businesses up to 20% of leads are ignored. The same studies show that prospects who have bothered to make contact frequently go on to become customers (up to 74% in one survey). What this says is that prospects who go to the trouble of contacting you virtually qualify themselves as hot leads. Yet the businesses they contacted often failed to pick up on the hint and lost the opportunity. Clearly, you cannot achieve sales unless you respond to leads—preferably rapidly. It is important to remember that in today's market, prospects may be more than 50% into their buyer's journey before they make contact with a salesperson which means that by the time they get to you they are often 'pre-qualified'.

Collateral Doesn't Win Business

If you are a salesperson who blames a lack of promotional material for a lack of sales, stop now. In all my years of B2B selling I never used promotional material in face-to-face engagement with prospective clients. Your role in B2B selling is to understand the client and what value you can deliver to them and their business. Using brochures, 'canned' slide shows and other prepared material instead focuses discussions around you, your product or service and company.

Managing Your Prospects

So now you have done the prospecting, qualified the opportunities and identified the real potential. To actively manage a prospect you need to be able to keep track of what's going on, report on opportunities and continually evaluate them.

In most businesses today, effective sales managers are using some form of CRM. These will help in managing your prospects, but I have also found keeping a track on my own leads has proven invaluable. Here are two popular ways to measure and manage your sales pipeline or sales funnel:

1. **The Gap Analysis**

   This is the most common and very simple method that involves:

   - considering your historical close rate—for example, you convert 20% of leads to sales

   - determining the average lead value—for example, $10,000

   - with a conversion rate of 20% you will multiply your target (say, $100,000) by 5, and so $500,000 (or 50 leads) need to be in your pipeline at any given time.

   The gap analysis is useful in its simplicity. However, it doesn't take into account lead times for the sales cycle, expected close dates and it does not reflect probability nor individual opportunities. It is used more often in commodity type sales.

2. Weighted Analysis

This method of managing your pipeline takes into account the progress you have made in developing the opportunity. Each opportunity is weighted by the probability of a conversion. For example, a $10,000 opportunity with a 50% chance of being sold has a weighted pipeline value of $10,000 x 0.5 =$5,000. The probability of conversion will vary from business to business so this is something you should explore with your sales manager. Below is a list of typical probabilities:

100%   **Contract finalised**

95%   **Letter of Intent received**

90%   **Acknowledged as preferred supplier. Timeframe for order placement confirmed.**

80%   **Favourable confirmation from decision maker**

60%   **Favourable confirmation from recommender.**

50%   **One of 2 possible suppliers. Favourable negotiations w/decision makers.**

30%   **Proposal submitted. One of 3 possible suppliers. Negotiation w/recommenders**

20%   **Client has confirmed decision timeframe. Your solution confirmed acceptable.**

10%   **Prospect needs identified, you are able to offer solution.**

Stage Three
Identify Needs

People usually buy for 2 reasons:
to ease pain, or
to achieve a gain

In this next stage of the sales cycle the salesperson needs to be determining how they can solve the problem a prospect might have, thereby *'easing their pain'*; or they need to work out how to generate more revenue or profit or customer satisfaction for the prospect, thereby *'delivering gain'*.

Alternatively the salesperson needs to be looking for ways to appropriately and confidently 'confront' the prospect to challenge their status quo.

**"My greatest strength as a consultant is to be ignorant
and ask a few questions"**
Peter Drucker (1909-2005), Austrian-born, American
management consultant

In recent times, there has been a lot of discussion amongst the commentators and influencers in the sales world about whether 'solution-based' and/or 'relationship-based' selling is still relevant. They are shining the spotlight rather on the new methodologies such as Insight and Challenger selling. Advocates of these methodologies both argue that with the propensity of information available to buyers in today's market, and the fact that buyers may be as far as 70% into their buying cycle before engaging with a salesperson, that the buyer has already worked out the solution without the help of a salesperson. Therefore, they argue that successful B2B salespeople should be going to prospects earlier in the buying journey and providing them with 'commercial insights' as to what is happening in the broader market and they should be 'teaching' and 'challenging' the way the prospect is currently doing business. But in each instance, there is no point in providing insights or challenging the status quo if you don't have a solution that addresses pain or gain. Likewise, developing a strong relationship based around the personal profile you have created will help you gain access to those most influential in any decision. Therefore, in my view, identifying the needs of the prospect and building relationships remain very important parts of the sales cycle.

It is a stage that consists of asking questions, uncovering needs, giving information about your product or service, and resolving how you might fulfil the prospects needs (refer back to 'Exploration' in the Buyer's Journey). You remain in a discovery phase of the sales cycle and you should not be afraid to acknowledge any gaps in your knowledge or understanding of the prospect's current situation and challenges. Asking for clarity and demonstrating your sincere wish to understand and help comes through in a positive way. Key to this is to use rapport building skills to engage the prospect, develop their trust and enable them to be open to talking to you about their business. All the while, you'll be listening carefully for the needs that they express and be thinking about how you can offer a solution to them. Don't hurry this stage. People are going to buy for their reason, not yours, so you need the time necessary to find out what those reasons are. You need to build a rapport with them and ask discovery questions.

Listening and questioning to discover needs

Success in this discovery phase depends on two basic skills—**active listening and creative questioning**. Good listening is one of the most important aspects of building a relationship (we covered this in Chapter 3). When you have a meeting with a prospect or client, you should be listening for perhaps 80% of the time. That's how you draw out a prospect's key concerns and gather more detail on areas that you may have only sketched in during your research. And, when you listen more than you talk, customers realise you are genuinely interested in them, and that you are trying to understand their specific situation. They feel more comfortable with you, and are more likely to open up.

If you are not moving closer to what you want, you probably aren't doing enough asking.
Jack Canfeld, American author of
'Chicken Soup For The Soul'

There are certain techniques you can use to encourage people to talk. The main one is to use open-ended questions. These are questions that start with 'how', 'why', 'which', 'who', 'when' or 'where'. They require an explanation rather than a yes or no answer so they provide a lot more information. It is also beneficial for you to present these questions in a way that positions you as understanding the prospect's market and business. For instance, as mentioned earlier, "I have noticed other businesses similar to yours are experiencing…as a result of…How is this impacting you?"

Another technique is to invite the client to prioritise the things they are looking for.

It is also important to restate, or paraphrase what you hear them tell you, so as to verify that you have understood correctly. You can use phrases like, *"Are you saying that…?"*, *"So that means…"* and *"What I am hearing you say is that…"* to solicit confirmation or correction of your understanding. This last technique is actually a coaching skill, and while there is a clear benefit to you in clarifying your understanding, it often also helps the prospect to get to the core of their issue. When having these conversations you lead a prospect to gaining more clarity about their own situation, they see in you the potential to be a trusted advisor.

It is usually quite easy for us to identify something that is causing us pain and that we want a solution for. However, identifying the prospect's need to ease pain is just one part of the process. Keep the conversation going so that you also understand what a 'solution' that provides greater opportunity (gain) looks like to them.

Now I Understand…

Through this time of building rapport, and using active listening and creative questioning you need to uncover the following essential information to:

- understand the prospect's business concerns, and how they make their buying decisions. This means you can now think of a tailor-made pitch for them;
- pick up on additional opportunities that could mean bigger or future sales;
- determine whether the prospect appreciates the risk of not taking up the challenge you may be presenting;
- look for areas where you may be able to up-sell or cross-sell during the sale—which may also help differentiate you so that you win the deal.

Cross-selling and up-selling

Cross-selling is selling other items from across your product or service range when a customer makes their initial purchase. Up-selling is making it attractive for the customer to purchase a bigger item or more of the initial item. A classic example of this is when the counterperson at McDonalds asks you: "Would you like fries with that?", or "Would you like to 'Super Size' that order?", that's cross-selling and up-selling in action. However, from just this perspective it can appear that you use cross-selling and up-selling simply to increase your average transaction value. That's not their sole purpose. They can play an important role in delivering excellent customer service and adding real value. Through cross-selling and up-selling you have opportunities to present guidance, options and information that your customer might not know. The aim is for cross-selling and up-selling to help you deliver optimal value to your customer and create a win/win outcome by ensuring a complete solution is offered and provided. This may involve ongoing maintenance or support in mission-critical applications, the introduction of partners to provide ancillary services or ensuring your solution is a 'future-proof' as possible so it meets expected growth in your client's business.

If you are looking to up-sell or cross-sell simply to increase your commission, you need to rethink! Not only is your motivation wrong, you will be minimising the opportunity for repeat business with this client.

Identifying cross-selling and up-selling opportunities

The best place to start setting up a cross-selling and up-selling system is to identify opportunities with your sales team members. Create a list of all your products and services, and for every item on list, ask:

• What else of value can we offer the customer to go with this purchase?

- What has been sold with this product or service in the past? Why? What added value did the client receive?

- What else could we offer that would add value or improve the use of this purchase?

- What else, when paired with this product or service, would help a customer get the most out of it?

- Are there partners we could introduce to provide a more complete, added-value solution?

Create cross-selling and up-selling checklists for each item on your sales inventory list and use this as a guide as to what to suggest during a sale.

Down-selling

Yes, it does exist and down-selling is an often overlooked sales tactic. It involves offering the prospect less than a complete solution as an entry-point in developing a longer-term relationship. Not to be confused with 'loss leader', down-selling is about giving the client something that helps them understand the value a relationship with your company could deliver. It's a bit like 'try before you buy'. In today's IT cloud-based market, this is becoming more common as businesses have the opportunity to implement in stages and 'test the water' before fully committing.

That said, it is important that the customer has investment in a 'try before you buy' approach. The customer must be committed to make a trial successful otherwise this approach is likely to fail.

Stage Four

Formulate and present solution

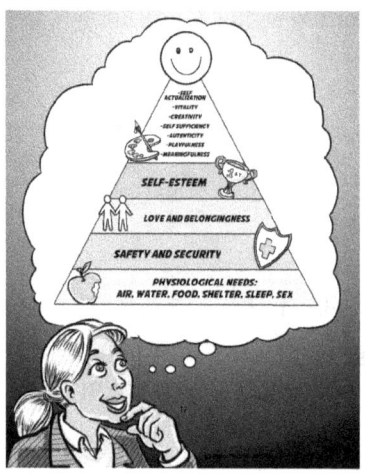

"The man who will use his skill and constructive
imagination to see how much he can give for a dollar,
instead of how little he can give for a dollar, is bound to
succeed"
Henry Ford (1863—1947), American industrialist and
founder of Ford Motor Co.

Addressing the prospect's needs

In this stage of the sales cycle, you use your knowledge and
understanding of the prospect's needs, as well as your knowledge
and experience in the industry or market and of your product or
service to formulate a proposal that will address their pain and/or
deliver a gain—to add value recognised by your prospect. It is at this

stage that some of the 'insight' and 'challenger' selling techniques can be useful and effective. Part of the solution we may want to offer the prospect may include helping them 'gain' as a result of you working with them in a consultative manner that unearths opportunities they haven't yet considered. But at the outset of this stage, it helps to first analyse the prospect's needs. We can get some help here from the psychologist, Abraham Maslow who defined a hierarchy of human needs

Maslow's Hierarchy of Needs

PERSONAL FULFILMENT

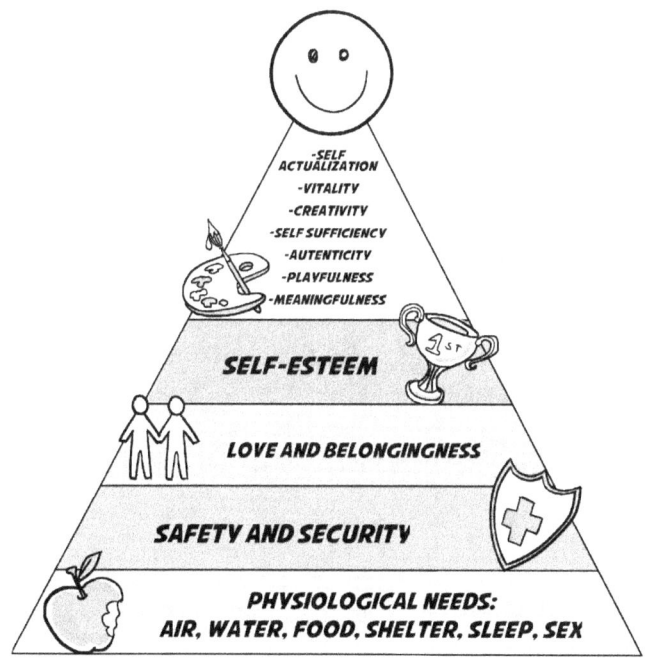

- SELF ACTUALIZATION
- VITALITY
- CREATIVITY
- SELF SUFFICIENCY
- AUTENTICITY
- PLAYFULNESS
- MEANINGFULNESS

SELF-ESTEEM

LOVE AND BELONGINGNESS

SAFETY AND SECURITY

PHYSIOLOGICAL NEEDS:
AIR, WATER, FOOD, SHELTER, SLEEP, SEX

SURVIVAL

Maslow identified five levels of needs, ranging from the most basic, which have to do with survival; to the highest needs, which have to do with personal fulfilment:

1. **Level one needs are physiological**—they relate to having enough food to eat, adequate shelter to keep out the elements, clothing to protect against heat and cold and enough time to sleep.

2. **Level two needs involve safety and security**—they relate to having a stable social structure where there are laws, where you can insure against disaster, and where you feel safe in your own home.

3. **Level three needs are social**—they relate to the need to feel loved, to have companionship, to be part of a community, and to have a place among family and friends.

4. **Level four needs involve status**—they relate to the need for recognition and respect, and the opportunity to be appreciated for achievements.

5. **Level five needs deal with self-actualization**—people meet needs on this level when they achieve their personal goals and ambitions, fulfil their potential and find personal meaning in their lives.

These 'needs' can be personal and/or business and the astute salesperson will be adept at understanding all areas of their prospects 'needs'.

How does the analysis of needs help you?

When you sell a client a benefit, you are pitching to at least one of Maslow's levels, and your approach needs to be appropriate to that level. The Hierarchy of Needs can help you to pinpoint the context of the prospect's need, and then position your solution at that same level.

It also enables you to target your solution at several, or at higher levels to increase its appeal to your prospect and give you a competitive edge.

Take this simple example. If you are selling rock climbing gear, it makes sense to pitch your communications at levels one and two, since the primary purpose of your gear is to keep the climber safe. The survival benefits of your rock climbing gear need to be clearly evident in your sales messages and marketing collateral. However, rock-climbing as a sport also speaks to higher levels of need such as status and self-actualisation. If you understand that your prospect wants a safe climb as priority, but it also very driven to achieve personal rock-climbing goals in pursuit of recognition and fulfilment, you are going to address multiple levels of needs in your presentation of your solution.

In a B2B environment, you may be offering a product or service that addresses an immediate and obvious need (levels 1 and 2), but also be able to deliver a significant increase in customer satisfaction, a unique competitive advantage or kudos for the decision maker (levels 4 and 5)

"The best sales questions have your expertise wrapped up in them"
Jill Konrath, American sales strategist, author and speaker.

Selling benefits, NOT features

It's a clichéd but very true phrase in sales "customers buy benefits, not features". All too often, salespeople get caught up in the features of their products or services, (especially, the Techo-type salesperson); and they make the mistake of selling from their own point of view, rather than from the prospect's perspective. In order to keep you focused on benefits, it helps to have conducted an analysis of your product or service's features and benefits, so that you are clear on the differences, and know better how to present benefits to your prospect. But also remember that a benefit for one person may be meaningless to another. So only present benefits that are relevant based on what you have learnt in your 'discovery'

Identifying product features

When selling products to consumers, the functional features may be important, but often secondary to aesthetics. In a B2B environment however, the opposite will normally be true.

"People don't want a quarter-inch drill, they want a quarter-inch hole"
Theodore Levitt (1925 - 2006), German born American economist and Harvard Business School professor.

So let's identify some simple product features and benefits from a more B2C perspective:

- Size
- Shape
- Texture
- Consistency
- Colour

For some products, visual appeal, taste or smell could also be relevant.

Translating product features to benefits

Having identified these features, how can these now be translated into benefits to the customer as long as your research has indicated it is important to them? A simple way to do this is to continually as "So what?"

- Small for portability and convenience
- Colour to fit mood or purpose

- Texture for feel or function
- Engineering for comfort and usability
- Quality is its own benefit
- Simplicity means 'easy to use'
- Durability and reliability
- Safety is a benefit, but may be a minimum requirement
- Style and design make goods desirable

Service features and benefits

Services also have features that translate into benefits that can meet your prospect's specific and unique needs, such as:

- Effective communications—saves time, improves integration of supply chain, keeps buyer informed
- Reliable/fast delivery—more time to enjoy benefits purchased
- Speed and reliability—less maintenance costs, greater throughput (revenue, profit)
- Top-notch customer service—knowing the 'sale' doesn't end with delivery or installation
- Highly qualified people—able to provide insight into industry
- Consistent supply and distribution—very important in mission critical situations, minimal downtime in event of failure

These examples are deliberately over-simplified to demonstrate the difference between features and benefits. The more complex the sale, the more specialised the solution, the more technical the offering and the more 'mission-critical' the deliverable, the more time and effort needs to be put into identifying the specific and tailored benefits of your features—what do these features represent in the eye of the buyer?

Better Still, Sell VALUE!

Focussing on the benefits you can deliver your prospect and client is essential in B2B selling, but you can take this to the next level by focussing on value.

Effective B2B salespeople make an effort to learn how their product or service delivers value to their prospective clients. What is happening in the industry that may trouble businesses, how can their product or service address this or help the prospect take advantage of emerging trends?

Value = What you get/What you give up

It all starts with the *'Voice of the Customer'*. All too often we, as salespeople or business managers think we know what the customer wants. But do we know what they value? In my experience the answer to that is a resounding 'MAYBE'.

Like beauty, value is in the eye of the beholder. The same feature of our product and benefit that it delivers, may be seen very differently by different customers. Ultimately, value is anything our client is prepared to pay for and the goal of a business (marketing and sales) is to clearly understand this from both a market and individual customer perspective...and this might not just be a financial transaction. Time is one of the most valuable things we have and getting prospective clients to spend time with us is a form of payment.

Having worked with thousands of businesses over the years, I have found there are some generic values desired by customers.

First is **Price**. I know there is a strong argument that people buy on value, not on price, but in many instances this is still where our buyers see 'value'. As our product or service becomes more and more commoditised, our customer will become more likely to make decisions based around the dollars that are exchanged and/or the time they must commit to the transaction. So while the price is so often seen as the monetary transaction, it may also relate to the ease of purchasing (ie time spent). Simply being the cheapest won't help if we haven't clearly understood that time (for example), is seen as value.

Quality is another 'simple' value that is often taken for granted. At any price-point there is an expected level of quality that is defined by the individual. As a general rule, quality is associated with price and the higher the price the better the quality expected. One error made by many businesses is not clearly understanding the level of quality expected at a price-point and either under-delivering (creating a poor customer experience) or over-delivering (generally at a cost to the business).

Communication—If we accept time is a valuable commodity, it follows that in simplifying communication and the time taken in the process, there is value being added. This can come in many forms—the time and speed of our responses to clients and the quality of documentation that we provide; not just with the product, but throughout the buying process. In the service industry this can be particularly important and can be a key differentiator between firms.

Packaging & Labelling. This is of particular importance if we are an integral part of our clients supply chain. While there is often a minimum requirement simply to be considered, improving our packaging and labelling to improve the logistics efficiencies of our clients, can separate us from competitors.

Many businesses value **Flexibility**. This can deliver significant value to your clients. This flexibility may, for example, be in payment terms, design, or in delivery. If our business is inflexible in creating flexibility for our clients, we are missing a significant opportunity to add value to the customer's experience.

Technical support and after-sales service is extremely valuable for some clients, especially those who have a critical reliance on the product or service you provide. Ongoing support is often the most significant criteria for buyers.

Recently I have seen businesses and consumers start to place more value on the **environmental credentials** of suppliers. For example, while many businesses in Australia breathed a sigh of relief when the carbon tax was repealed, others had already experienced the benefits, both from a marketing and operational perspective and saw the value this translated to in terms of marketing and productivity.

By using the table below, both for your product/service generically and for each opportunity, you can:

1. Identify the significant features of your product or service (or a packaged solution you are offering)

2. Assess how these features translate into benefits.

3. Start to translate the benefits into value the buyer will see delivered.

Product/Service	Features	Benefits	Value
1.			
2.			
3.			
4.			
5.			
6.			
7.			
8.			

While the above table is useful from a generic perspective (ie what does your product or service offer in a broad sense), as you work with specific opportunities, the column 'Product/Service' can be replaced with 'Customer Needs' and then identify what feature of your offering addresses this need and what specific benefit will the prospect receive by implementing you offering—what **value** does it create for your customer? Remember to keep asking yourself— "So what?"

Knowing your competition

If you also know and understand the features and benefits of competing products or services, you will also be able to find the ways to position your offer as 'the one' to deliver the value most important to your prospect.

A mentor of mine in my early days of sales once told me to learn the strengths and weaknesses of my competitors as well as my own. Only then could I be ready to counter the competitor's strengths and emphasise their weaknesses while ensuring I was delivering real value to the prospect.

"Know your enemy and know yourself and you can fight a hundred battles without disaster"
Sun Tsu

Making the shift from USP to a Value Proposition

Working out your Unique Selling Proposition (USP) used to be a fundamental part of this sales cycle stage of formulating your solution. But that has all changed. Nowadays, by the time you have defined your USP, it is most likely that it will no longer be unique. Furthermore, when it comes to uniqueness, customers don't care. In today's business world, 'unique' is not only difficult to define and explain with any level of credibility, it has a very short life-span. Some may think this is controversial, especially more traditional or academically-focused marketers, but it's a fact—*customers don't care if you are unique, they only care about the value you deliver.*

In 'real-world' marketing and sales, you are usually competing with businesses that are similar to you that deliver products or services that are similar to yours too. Claiming uniqueness is risky and difficult to justify. Your time would be better spent on showing prospects and clients the value you deliver.

Your USP is said to be the factor or factors that differentiate you, your product or service, or your company from the competition. First proposed in the 1960's by advertising pioneer, Rosser Reeves, the premise is to focus on 'what you have that your competitors don't'. But in today's fast-paced world, even if you have a patent or are market-leading in the introduction of a product, it will soon be copied in a manner that dilutes the competitive advantage that your 'uniqueness' briefly offered.

What may make you unique today is easily and quickly replicated by competitors. Even your own business may cannibalise its uniqueness as you strive to stay ahead of the pack by quickly releasing new products and updating the old (think about Apple's iPhone and what it did to the iPod!) In working to define a USP you are internally focussed, looking at what you think makes you different and/or better than your competitors. But if this difference is not important to the prospect, it is of no consequence.

Your value proposition, on the other hand, is externally focused, and it explains how your product or service solves problems or improves situations. It is specific to the benefits you deliver, and it explains why your prospects should consider you over your competitors. It can be defined as 'the extent to which a product or service is perceived by your customer as meeting their needs or wants, measured by their willingness to pay for it'. It depends more on the customer's perception of the worth of the product than on its cost or uniqueness.

There are two types of value propositions that need to be clarified—your generic value proposition for a specific target market and secondly, your value proposition for a specific opportunity. You use the first to open doors but then it is important that you put that aside, conduct your discovery and then generate your opportunity specific value proposition. First we will discuss the generic value proposition.

Your generic value proposition statement needs to:

- identify/confirm your target market and ideal client

- be expressed *from a customer's point of view*

- demonstrate your understanding of your prospect's environment and how they will use your product or service

- define the most important benefits, not the features, as they would be experienced by your customers

- specifically articulate what gain you deliver and what pain do you remove

Test your generic value proposition statement

You might think you have a great value proposition, but you don't count. A value proposition is only of benefit to you and your company if it resonates with, and is seen as believable by your ideal client. Going forward, regularly review and revise your value proposition. Your market won't stand still and your customers won't wait—continually assess where you stand in your market.

By focusing on *value* and not what you think makes you *different,* you are more likely to win customers. Understanding what customers value shows you are in synch with their wants and needs, even if they may not yet know what they want themselves.

"If I'd asked what they wanted, they'd have said a faster horse."
Henry Ford (1863—1947), American industrialist and
founder of Ford Motor Co

If you focus on value, as defined by your customer, your R&D, marketing, sales and entire operations can be more focused meaning less wasted time, effort and money; and as a result greater profits and more satisfied customers.

I am not discounting here the value that uniqueness can deliver. Just be mindful of where uniqueness has the most value. In today's fast-moving sales environment, the uniqueness should be YOU, your sales process and your customer support—these should form the customer experience of culture of your business. Culture cannot be copied, and it will set you apart.

Ultimately, only a small percentage of your target market may be 'early-adopters', attracted by the uniqueness of your 'first-mover' advantage. Fewer still will be attracted by the uniqueness of your brand, although in luxury markets this is seen as value—just ask Kim Kardashian. In the real world, it's not who does it first, or who is the only one that does it. It's who does it best for the customer that counts. What is of interest to your market is the value they receive from what you offer.

Things to remember when presenting your solution

You've done your analysis. You have defined the benefits you offer and your opportunity specific value proposition. You know what you are going to put on the table, and you're ready to present your solution that you feel confident will meet your prospect's needs; and this may occur several times throughout the sales cycle.

Here are a few tips:

Have an agenda

Let those attending know the purpose of the presentation meeting (or any meeting throughout the sales cycle). The agenda should be relevant and focused on the customer, not you. Every meeting should create value for the customer. Here's a simple format:

1. Introductions
2. Meeting objective and timeframes
3. Prospect's need (or challenge you are making to the status quo)—Present back to the prospect their challenge or opportunity. Make sure you confirm and emphasise this so you gain their attention
4. Value proposition—summarise the benefits the prospect believe they will receive by implementing your solution…as they have defined and you have identified during your sales cycle and then present the value proposition.
5. Your plan—What will you deliver, how and when, to address the challenge/opportunity of the prospect?
6. Company background—keep this brief. Let them know they are dealing with a reliable business
7. Confirm—make sure you ask what questions/uncertainties they might have. Does your proposal meet their expectations? Is there anything you have missed? What are the next steps?

Know your audience

Always ask for the names and roles of the people who will be attending your presentation. Be aware of any attendees who have not been involved in your discussions to date and research their backgrounds before the meeting. Are there any 'hidden' decision makers? In many smaller businesses and start-ups you may find that external investors, silent partners (including spouses) may have more of a say than you have been able to determine during your journey to date with your prospect.

Ensure you are presenting the right solution to the right person

Know the community of influence. Salespeople are told to personalise their offerings. Right? Well, maybe not. Often there are 'lurkers' in the decision-making unit, and if these players have not been identified, a proposal that is too personalised for one decision-maker risks alienating the 'lurkers'.

Always 'present' your proposal

In some situations, like tender responses, there is no alternative but to 'drop off' the proposal. As far as possible, request a meeting to deliver the proposal so you can highlight how your offer will impact their business and address any immediate questions they may have. It is vital to read the body language and get your customers feedback.

Know what you are really selling

Your prospect wants to buy a solution to a problem or a tool/service that will help grow their business. Make sure you understand what they see as value and highlight this in your proposal. Emphasise the things that make you different, more superior to the known competitors and the resulting differentiated value for the customer. Do not discuss product details or benefits that are not applicable or relevant to the customer.

Use the right language

I am not speaking of English, French or German, but of the need to keep the language of your proposal and presentation relevant to the audience. This is not a time to demonstrate that you know all the latest buzzwords and industry jargon. It's a time to use language relevant to the individuals to whom the proposal is targeted. In more complex sales, there will often be a need to provide technical details that will form part of performance evaluation and this may well require the use of more technical language—after all, it will be reviewed by people who expect it and understand. The message here is 'be relevant' and avoid 'bafflegab'.

Don't over-promise

Don't oversell yourself. Remember that after closing the deal you will have to live up to the expectations you set to keep the relationship alive. If you set great expectations and then fall even a little bit short you will be judged in a negative way. In terms of building a relationship and maintaining your credibility, it's better to be sure that you can not only meet, but perhaps, exceed expectations you have set up.

Check how it's going

As you will have done throughout the sales cycle, it works to your advantage to actively seek feedback from your prospect during your presentation. Regularly checking in with your prospect changes a pitch from a one-way street and keeps your relationship-building conversation going with the prospect. Asking questions such as *'How does that seem so far?'*, and *'Are there any doubts, concerns, issues or areas for improvement so far?'* can elicit important answers to guide you through the remainder of the pitch. Raising questions like *'What would we need to do to make this solution part of the way you do business?'* or *'Is there something you would change about your current supplier?'* can deepen your insights in a moment, allow for flashes of inspiration and enable you to incorporate the prospect's wishes into your bid. Having a strong, trusted relationship is essential to being able to engage in these conversations and be confident you are getting open and honest responses.

While I have shown the presentation as a single step in this sales cycle, in reality there will often be many presentations throughout the engagement with your prospect. How many, how complex and who will be involved will change throughout the journey and will depend on the type of sale in which you are engaged. Regardless, the points I have covered here will be appropriate in some form and should be clearly understood and practised

Stage Five
Provide Answers

In many sales cycles this stage is often referred to as 'Handle Objections', assuming that the solution you have presented has real or perceived 'loop-holes'. However, if you are managing the sales cycle in a professional way, you will be in an ongoing dialogue with the prospect and their response to your presentation of a solution is more likely to take the form of questions along the way rather than objections at the end.

A prospect's feedback at this stage, whether in the form of questions or objections, is truly valuable to you. As well as the immediate need to provide answers to help progress the current sale, feedback provided at this crucial stage provides you with vital insights into both the perceptions of your market and the individuals you need to engage with. It gives you important clues as to how your business thinking, your relationship-building and presentation skills are perceived. For instance, a prospect who questions the track record of your company at this stage is telling you they need more solid information about the sustained performance of your company; and a prospect who questions the quality of your product or service is telling you that they need more evidence that your solution works. Reflecting thoroughly on the types of questions you get from prospects; and their demeanour in response to a proposal you have presented, can show you just where and how improvements can be made by you, the salesperson, and your company. Fully appreciating this stage of the sales cycle, and making it work for you, is very important so that you don't fall into taking on a defensive, a disappointed or an impatient mode, which can fell all the rapport you have been building.

"It's easier to explain price once than to apologize for quality forever"
Zig Ziglar (1926—2012), American author, sales guru and motivational speaker

---

If you are faced with questions, or objections:

- welcome them gratefully; be aware that this prospect is doing you a favour by adding a new depth to your knowledge and experience through voicing their concerns

- realise that you need to develop a set of responses that pre-empt objections, you can deliver convincingly, that can legitimately neutralise objections and keep the discovery dialogue going

- let the prospect elaborate fully and feel sure they have been heard; don't cut them off, dismiss them or divert them with tactics such as finishing their sentences for them

- make sure you fully understand their doubts or reservations; restate and paraphrase to confirm your understanding of their concerns
- don't retaliate by debating, arguing or pointing out where 'they are wrong'
- treat a prospect's concerns as fully legitimate; and use them to constructively continue to build the relationship and demonstrate your ability to be a trusted advisor
- ask questions with the aim of drilling down to the real issue, adding value to the prospect
- provide facts or experiences about your product or service to back up your claims
- refer back to the problem they identified and reiterate your solution
- fully explore how changing timelines and financing terms or even, offering different testimonials may work in your favour
- confirm you have overcome the objection and, if necessary, make the 'ask' again

Remember, if the prospect is prepared to spend time with you in dialogue about your proposal, it would be a rare individual that would be wasting their time and yours if they were not interested in what you have proposed.

"Obstacles are necessary for success because in selling, as in all careers of importance, victory comes only after many struggles and countless defeats."
Og Mandino (1923—1996), American author of
'The Greatest Salesman in the World'

When to back out

You need to know when to back out of a deal. Even in these final stages of a sales cycle, it can happen that it only becomes clear that your product or service really doesn't meet client needs or that your business focus is elsewhere. In that case, you have to say so. Don't hesitate to do this; you will actually gain a lot of credibility. You will keep the door open to come back sometime in the future and win a deal that really suits both you and the client. You might also want to back out if alarm bells clang at this stage. For instance, it may dawn on you that the costs of doing business with this prospect will outweigh the benefits. Perhaps, they don't have the budget to afford what you really want to deliver. Or perhaps your gut feeling tells you that they are likely to be difficult or unreliable, or not able to implement effectively and therefore become a poor or risky reference. In these cases, you should back out before you make further investments of your time and energy.

Confirm the Sale

If you have done your job well by focusing on building trust, making sure that there is a good fit between you and the prospect, and clearly articulating the real value that you offer from the customer's perspective, you will rarely hear a 'no' as you move on to the stage of confirming the sale. Mostly, it comes as a natural progression of a process of discovery, relationship-building and the realisation of mutual benefit that actually doesn't require you to do anything more than be available to make the confirmation in partnership with the prospect. That's why I term this stage as the 'confirmation of the sale' versus the more aggressive 'closing of the sale', which is often associated with more manipulative sales techniques. The beauty of going through this type of sales cycle is that it leads naturally to a 'yes'.

> **"You don't close a sale; you open a relationship if you
> want to build a long-term, successful enterprise."**
> Patricia Fripp, American sales trainer and speaker

Successful salespeople question, qualify and address issues throughout the sales cycle to arrive at a seamless confirmation of the sale. However, there will be certain sales processes (usually transactional or commodity-based) where this doesn't work or is less applicable and, in these instances a 'close' is required.

In these situations there are several techniques you can use in the process of confirming the business. For instance you can:

- leverage key influencers to help the prospect make a decision

- propose a specific timeframe for your offer to give a sense of urgency

- refer back to the problem they identified, reiterate your solution and stress the cost of NOT proceeding

There are also a few techniques you can employ to get the prospect set-up for confirmation:

- assuming the close—"So, can we say this will…"

- creating a balance sheet—List 10 benefits and then ask the prospect to name the negatives

- providing a choice—"Would you like delivery Monday or…"

- exploring the costs of delaying the decision

- elaborating on benefits—"I can see I haven't explained this properly. Can we go through all the benefits and see which one is stopping us proceeding?"

- return of serve—"Does it come in black?" "Would you like it in black?" If they answer yes, close.

These are some of the common mistakes I have seen transactional salespeople make at this stage:

- not asking for the order
- too many distractions
- not in the mood to sell
- talking too much
- rushing the close
- loss of control

Implementation

You've confirmed the sale, but your work is not over with this new client. You now have to safeguard your relationship with them and continue to build their trust. Use your internal network to ensure that delivery happens as you said it would. Follow up directly with the client to get their feedback.

As mentioned in describing the 'Buyer's Journey', all too many salespeople think the sale is over once a contract is signed or an order received. Successful salespeople know this is not the case and while it will vary product-to-product, market-to-market and business-to-business, you should maintain interest in the implementation of what you have sold to ensure your customer receives what they expect.

Stage Eight
Follow-up and start again

One always hopes that things go according to plan, but they don't always. Don't avoid client complaints, be proactive about them. For instance, if things have gone wrong, you need acknowledge problems and apologise, even if you are not the one who is directly responsible, and also express your regret. Always let clients vent if that's what they want to do. Don't cut them off, argue, defend or try to counter their communication. Make sure that you give them the time, space and attention so that they feel heard. Then, take immediate action to remedy the problem, and give the client regular feedback as to your progress. Aim to surprise the client with how well you meet their concerns and get the relationship back on track. This will build trust and help to cement your relationship. But this does not suggest you should accept unreasonable demands or unwarranted claims. The customer is NOT always right, but they need to feel their issues are taken seriously and receive due consideration.

"If you are not taking care of your customers, your competitor will"
Bob Hooey, Canadian sales trainer and speaker

You need to continue to follow up and maintain regular contact with this client, deepening the relationship over time and developing all the time as a trusted and valued advisor to them. Even if there are others in your organisation that take on the 'farming' role, successful salespeople still maintain client relationships to ensure that future opportunities are not missed, that referrals can be generated and networks nurtured as they return to Step 1, Lead Generation.

Epilogue
Miscellaneous thoughts to help you become a better salesperson

Motivating Mind Games

Staying motivated is the 'inner game' you play to maintain a positive attitude, and achieve sales success:

- *Positive expectations*—expecting the best is key to a positive, optimistic attitude

- *Positive self-talk*—coach yourself to success with encouraging self-talk

- *Positive imaging*—use 'mental rehearsal' before each sales call and see your success happen

- *Positive mental food*—feed your mind with books, webinars, podcasts and other digital content, as well as seminars and presentations

- *Positive people*—associate with other winners

- *Positive personal development and training*—become a lifelong student of your profession

---

"The difference between try and triumph is just a little umph!"
Marvin Phillips—credited to Marvin Phillips,
American author

Seven Questions that get to the Essence of Planning

1. What results do I intend to achieve?
2. What must I do to get those results?
3. What are the priorities among the activities?
4. How much time does each activity require?
5. When will I execute each activity?
6. How much flexibility do I have for the unexpected?
7. What does NOT need to be done?

The 30/60/90 Day Work Plan

This is a template you can use to develop 30, 60 or 90 Day plans. This gives you short enough time-frames so you can see the results, and it is long enough to allow you to make the objective worthwhile. For larger projects, you can use a Rolling 90 Day Plan.

There are four good reasons to set 30/60/90-Day objectives:

1. To identify what you want to accomplish
2. To help you focus on what matters most
3. To make sure that you and your team/manager/family are in agreement regarding your priorities
4. To provide you with accountability

You can use the following template to develop your most important or urgent goals as a miniature work plan that can be achieved in 30, 60 or 90 days

1. Now: What is the current problem/situation?

_____

_____

_____

_____

2. Goal: What do you want to achieve, and by when?

_____

_____

_____

_____

3. How: List three or four most essential stages to achieve this goal and give completion dates for each stage.

_____

_____

_____

_____

4. Resources: What or who do you need to make this happen?

_____

_____

_____

_____

5. Trouble-shooting: What are the possible roadblocks, and how will you get around them?

_____

_____

_____

_____

6. Actions: List the actual activities and the time-lines necessary to make this happen

_____

_____

_____

_____

7. Measurement: What is the benchmark that tells you that you have achieved the goal?

_____

_____

_____

_____

> **"People with goals succeed because they know where they're going."**
> Earl Nightingale (1921—1989), American radio
> personality, writer, speaker and author,

Here are a few tips to help you in your planning process:

Triple A Planning:

- Aims—your goals or objectives
- Activities—define all the stages of the process of reaching the goal
- Action Plans—the actual steps and timelines necessary to make it happen

FAI—Forecast, Audit & Innovate

- Forecast is the answer to the questions, what does the future look like or what would you like it to look like?

- Audit is the assessment of where you are actually to determine the gap between your present reality and the forecast

- Innovate is to come up with the things you have to do to realize the opportunity or improved situation

10. Steps to Deal with Sales Droughts

Tough times in sales are inevitable. No matter how well you have planned; there will be times when you are struggling to make targets.

Here are some insights to help you:

1. Find out the root causes of the problems—Has something changed with your product or service? Has there been a shift in the market? Etc

2. Don't give up calling on prospects and customers even though they're in no mood or position to buy. *During the GFC I encouraged my clients to maintain appropriate, non-intrusive contact with their key clients and prospects. As the world economies emerged from the doom and gloom, these businesses were well positioned to quickly re-engage and understand the key issues facing their markets.*

3. Think through what you're doing. When conditions change, you have to change along with them.

4. Keep up your spirits. Harness your inner reservoirs of determination and resilience.

5. Fight harder and smarter for the accessible business and explore new territories.

6. Avoid panic. This is no time to make wholesale changes to how you approach your market without careful consideration.

7. Improve efficiency.

8. Broaden your viewpoint and investigate selling to other industries and through additional channels.

9. Treat good times as bad. Always deliver the level of service to your clients and build your opportunities as if you were in times of need. This will ensure you are always well positioned to meet downturns more positively

10. Remember that forecasting is part reason, part educated guess, part experience, part being a good listener, and all hard work. Nobody's forecast is right all the time, make the best assessment based on all the available facts, then work hard to make that guess come true.

"Obstacles don't have to stop you. If you run into a wall, don't turn around and give up. Figure out how to climb it, go through it, or work around it."
Michael Jordan (1963—), American former professional basketball player and businessman

---

20. Questions to Help You Grow Sales

I often work with clients who are really struggling to come up with ideas to generate new sales leads and improve their conversion rates. I use the following **20 questions** to help them hone in on what's going wrong and work out what they can do to turn things around.

For every **NO** that you answer, you are probably missing out on **OPPORTUNITIES** and that means **SALES.**

1. Can you name the three main things that set you apart from your competition?

2. Do you understand how to communicate the benefits of your product or service and the **value** it can deliver? Or are you too interested in telling people about the features?

3. Have you tried direct marketing to attract new customers? Did you accurately measure the results?

4. Do you 'think outside the box' with your direct marketing and warming up cold calls or do you just use 'same old, same old'??

5. Have you developed a strong personal brand and do you keep it up to date?

6. When you speak to a potential new customer, do you use words that set you apart from the rest that immediately capture the customer's attention?

7. Do you actively build your network both on and off-line?

8. Do you use social media to learn about your prospects and markets?

9. Do you send regular and relevant (valuable) communications to your customers and prospective customers?

10. Do you commit time and money on learning sales skills or getting advice on how to improve your sales?

11. Do you have a formal lead generation process in place?

12. Do you set up an ongoing communication with qualified leads consisting of phone calls, letters and emails? I call this getting them on the 'Buyer's Journey'

13. Do you obtain and use testimonials from your best customers?

14. Do you have a formal referrals system in place?

15. Do you actively look for triggers and challenges within your target market that may create opportunity to engage with clients and prospects?

16. Your clients' birthdays plus other personal details can be the most important piece of marketing information you can have and use! Do you have them?

17. Do you know the best way to sell is to ask questions? Do you do it?

18. Do you take exceptional care of your current customers? Do you WOW them?

19. Did you know that if you follow up a mail out with a phone call you can increase response rates by over 100%

20. Do you continually look to develop your sales skills, learn from others or engage a mentor?

Pick just three of the above questions that are important to you and take some action today to improve those areas. Don't delay and leave it another day.

The Critical Skills and Abilities for Successful Salespeople

- Good time management
- Comprehensive knowledge of the value your product or service delivers
- Critical thinking skills
- Excellent communication skills
- High self-awareness
- Well-developed empathy for others
- Good organizational ability
- Good conflict resolution skills
- Good negotiating skills
- Good problem-solving skills
- Knowledge of the market

Reading List

Over the years there have been a myriad of sales books written, some have become evergreen classics, others have provided guidance on the latest trends in selling and then faded away.

It is difficult to make generic recommendations as each of you reading this book will be in a different stage of your sales career. Some will be entering sales for the first time, others will be ascending to higher level, more complex sales. You will want to understand and improve specific areas of your personal sales skills.

As I have suggested throughout this book, to be successful you need to continue to learn. The following books have provided me guidance at some stage of my career. Research these books for those that are most applicable to your immediate needs and continue your journey of discovery in sales.

- **Your Roadmap to Sales Management Success*** by Wayne Moloney.

  Part of the author's 'Roadmap to Business Success' series, this is a practical handbook for those aspiring to, or new to sales management; or simply those needing a refresh on the fundamentals of sales management.

- **The Joshua Principle***—Leadership Secrets of Selling by Tony J Hughes.

  Tony shares the story of a young B2B salesperson who has fallen on hard times and how he is mentored to success discovering the 'secrets' to successful strategic selling along the way.

- **The Challenger Sale** by Brent Adamson and Matthew Dixon.

  Based on an exhaustive study of thousands of sales reps across multiple industries and geographies, The Challenger Sale argues that classic relationship building is a losing approach, especially when it comes to selling complex, large-scale business-to-business solutions.

- **The Challenger Customer** by Brent Adamson and Matthew Dixon.

  The follow-up to the Challenger Sale and again based on significant research, this book explores selling to the hidden influencers in any organisation to multiply your chances of success.

- **New Sales Simplified** by Mike Weinberg

  Great handbook on prospecting and new business development

- **SPIN Selling** by Neil Rackham

  Situation, Problem, Implication, Need-payoff—this classic is a must-read for any B2B salesperson

- **Smarter Selling*** by Keith Dugdale

  How to grow sales by building trusted relationships to better engage clients, spot opportunities and deliver additional value.

- **The Sales Bible** by Jeffrey Gitomer

  An evergreen sales manual that dissects the sales process and helps you reach your sales potential

- **Selling the Invisible** by Harry Beckworth

  Selling services is often a challenge to those used to product sales. This book provides practical advice on selling services and intangibles. A little dated, but still relevant.

- **The OneTEAM Method*** by Peter Strohkorb.

  Strictly speaking not a sales book but a book about how Sales and Marketing (and Product Management) can boost sales by better supporting each other

- **Rebirth of the Salesman*** by Cian Mcloughlin

  This book gets to the heart of the question every salesperson and sales leader wants to better understand: "As salespeople, why do we really win and lose and what can we do about it?" In this book you'll find the answers to this and many other perplexing sales questions.

- **One Minute Salesperson** by Spencer Johnson

  Johnson claims it's not about 'selling', it's about 'helping people', and shows how to do it successfully.

- **How to Master the Art of Selling** by Tom Hopkins

  One of the 'showmen' of sales training and motivation shares selling 'secrets' from some on the highest paid salespeople.

- **Selling 101** by Zig Ziglar

  Considered by many to be the 'must read' sales manual for anyone looking at sales as a career.

- **Customer Centered Selling** by Robert L Jolles

  Jolles focuses on the need to be actively involved in the buying process and offers an 8-step process to help you achieve this.

- **Non-Manipulative Selling** by Anthony Alessandra & Phillip Wexler

  A great read on how to go about building relationships with customers and how to do it without "selling" (in the traditional sense)

- **Customer Loyalty, How to Earn It, How to Keep It** by Jill Griffin

  Shares ideas and tactics to create loyal customers who will not only be repeat buyers, but advocates.

- **The Art Of Commercial Conversations***—When It's Your Turn to Make A Difference by Bernadette McClelland.

  Bernadette taps into what REALLY contributes to business success when it comes to *revenue generation, day-to-day leadership* and the *critical activation of those results that matter the most.*

- **Secrets of Question Based Selling** by Thomas A Freese

  Explores what we all should know in selling, asking questions that people want to answer and help you progress the sales process.

- **Why Customers Come Back** by Manzie R. Lawfer

  Shares ways to help you increase your retention rates and give your clients a reason to come back.

- **How to Sell and Manage in Tough Times and Tough Markets** by Tom Reilly

  Practical tips and advice on how salespeople and managers can effectively steer their way through times.

- **Snap Selling** by Jill Konrath

  With it becoming more and more difficult to get time with your prospects, this book shares ideas to speed up sales and win more business

- **Selling to Big Companies** by Jill Konrath

  Strategies and tactics to win more business from big business

- **Influence** by Robert Cialdini

  One of the classics on persuasion and why people say 'yes'

- **Predictably Irrational** by Dan Ariely.

  More psychology really, but very good exploring why we make irrational decisions and how to break through these thought processes

- **How to Win Friends and Influence People** by Dale Carnegie.

  Old and much maligned but a classic and still relevant in today's business environment

- **To Sell is Human** by Daniel Pink

  Defined as a modern-day 'How to Win Friends and Influence People'—Pink argues that we are all salespeople at some time and provides ideas on how to present your message more persuasively, better understand other's perspectives and sell more successfully

- **The Go Giver** by Bob Burg & John David Mann

  A story about "Joe" and how changing his focus from 'getting' to 'giving'—putting others' interests first and continually adding value to their lives—ultimately leads to unexpected returns.

- **Sales Leadership 2016—11 Sales Thought Leadership Perspectives*** by Sales Masterminds Australasia Collective

  Australasia's leading sales experts from the Sales Masterminds Australasian group have collaborated here to share their cutting-edge ideas and strategies to inspire, educate and empower sales professionals.

- **Combo Prospecting*** by Tony J. Hughes

  Brings timeless principles of success together with modern engagement tools and techniques... people and technology, social and the phone, insight and value, relationships and strategy.

- **strategicsellinggroup.com**

  Not a book but an invaluable resource for any B2B salespesron. John Smibert shares videos, interviews and other resources to help you grow and manage sales.

Set Yourself up for Success

Cultivate a keen, honest awareness of your strengths and weaknesses when it comes to the skills and competencies required by managers. Make it a habit to take time to reflect on how you just handled a situation or person or event. Ask for feedback from your managers and your team members, rather than relying on just your self-evaluation. Define your own areas for improvement; devise, commit to and implement a development plan that may include informal mentoring, coaching and training.

The stakes are high in sales and the stressors can be extreme. However, that's matched by even richer rewards. You want to be a winner in this field. Sales is a high impact career, and working towards consistently operating at the highest level of effectiveness will bring you an extraordinary sense of personal fulfilment.

Good luck...you are on a journey that will be one of the best you can take.

"Continuous effort—not strength or intelligence—is the key to unlocking our potential." *Winston Churchill*

About the Author

Wayne Moloney is a business strategist who lives in the Blue Mountains of NSW, Australia with his wife and children.

With a passion for sales, marketing and business development, Wayne has enjoyed a career spanning 40 years and the continents of Australia, Asia and Europe, and has held leadership positions in these areas, as well as in the roles of General Manager and Managing Director.

Wayne's experience in managing and growing businesses is not constrained by industry. With a belief that business management and sales development are processes that transcend the specificity of a product and service, he has successfully applied his principles to businesses as diverse as construction, fluids handling, manufacturing, pollution control, software development, telecommunications, education and many more.

'Your Roadmap to Achieving Sales Success' is the second in Wayne Moloney's series of *Business Roadmap* guides to sales, marketing and small business management. His first book, *'Your Roadmap to Sales Management Success'* is available on Amazon.

Connect with Wayne

Linked In
au.linkedin.com/in/waynemoloney

Twitter
@waynemoloney

You Tube
youtube.com/c/WayneMoloney

Google+
https://plus.google.com/u/0/+WayneMoloney

Facebook
https://www.facebook.com/Businessgrowthspecialist

Email
wayne@waynemoloney.com

Website
www.waynemoloney.com